The
Decorated Page

The Decorated Page

Journals, Scrapbooks & Albums
Made Simply Beautiful

Gwen Diehn

LARK BOOKS

A Division of Sterling Publishing Co., Inc.
New York

For

Mary Daugherty

Editor: **Joanne O'Sullivan**
Art Director: **Celia Naranjo**
Photography: **Evan Bracken**
Cover Design: **Barbara Zaretsky**
Assistant Editor: **Rain Newcomb**
Art Production Assistant:
Shannon Yokeley
Editorial Assistance: **Dana Lade**
Delores Gosnell

Library of Congress has cataloged the hardcover edition as follows:

Diehn, Gwen, 1943-
    The decorated page : journals, scrapbooks & albums made simply beautiful / by Gwen Diehn.
       p. cm.
    Includes index.
       ISBN 1-57990-299-5
    1. Photograph albums. 2. Photographs--Conversion and restoration. 3. Scrapbooks. 4. Scrapbooks--Design. I. Title.

    TR465 .D53 2002
    745.593--dc21

                                                        2002016218

10 9 8 7 6 5

Published by Lark Books, a division of
Sterling Publishing Co., Inc.
387 Park Avenue South, New York, N.Y. 10016

First Paperback Edition 2003
© 2002, Gwen Diehn

Distributed in Canada by Sterling Publishing,
c/o Canadian Manda Group, 165 Dufferin Street
Toronto, Ontario, Canada M6K 3H6

Distributed in the U.K. by:
Guild of Master Craftsman Publications Ltd.
Castle Place, 166 High Street Lewes East Sussex, England BN7 1XU
Tel: (+ 44) 1273 477374 Fax: (+ 44) 1273 478606
Email: pubs@thegmcgroup.com, Web: www.gmcpublications.com

Distributed in Australia by Capricorn Link (Australia) Pty Ltd.,
P.O. Box 704, Windsor, NSW 2756 Australia

If you have questions or comments about this book, please contact:
Lark Books
67 Broadway
Asheville, NC 28801
(828) 253-0467

Manufactured in China

ISBN 1-57990-299-5 (hardcover) 1-57990-512-9 (paperback)

For information about custom editions, special sales, premium and corporate purchases, please contact Sterling Special Sales Department at 800-805-5489 or special-sales@sterlingpub.com.

CONTENTS

INTRODUCTION

Keeping a journal is truly a journey. The very words come from a common root: the Old French word *journee* meaning "day." A journey originally meant the distance traveled in a day; a journal was a book in which one would record a day's events.

The beginning of any journey can be full of excitement and promise, but it can also be full of trepidation. What a beginning journaler fears most is an expanse of clean, white paper. And the only thing more intimidating than one sheet of clean white paper is a collection of sheets of clean, white paper, especially if they're nicely bound into a handsome book.

"My friend gave me this beautiful handmade journal," you explain, "but I can't bear to ruin it by writing or drawing in it!" Or, "I actually have a whole collection of blank books, and as soon as I figure out how to do something worthy of them, I'll start to write in them." Meanwhile, your collection grows, and with each new addition it becomes more intimidating, because now it's not only a single book, but a whole shelf full of perfectly clean and perfectly empty books.

Seeking inspiration and a cure for creative block, you may turn to a book about how to make journals or memory books. Glowing examples of layered richness, beautiful calligraphy, and intricate artwork leap from the pages. But how did the pages get that way? Mysterious processes involving obscure materials (and accompanying explanations that assume a high level of technical know-how) seem to be the key to creating these delicious pages: "Simply generate the type and image on a computer, then make a polymer plate and print it on an antique letterpress," or "You can create the effect shown here by painting in encaustic over an inscribed surface." Instead of helping you, the book only increases your trepidation. Your blank books remain blank, but now they are joined on the shelf by the beautiful book about journalmaking.

But it *is* possible to easily and quickly create pages that sing and weep, inform and beguile, transport, soothe, and excite. This book will show you simple processes you can use to fill the pages of your journals, scrapbooks, and albums with visual elements that enhance the written words and communicate facts, emotions, moods, and stories.

Ann Turkle's careful attention to detail is expressed in her closely observed and annotated sketches and narrative accounts of sheep in the Irish countryside.

My first experiment with creating a rich and expressive journal was when I was in college in San Antonio, Texas. In biology class, our assignment was to keep a journal about the ecology of a particular tree on the campus, recording and explaining interactions between the tree and its environment throughout the semester. I selected an orange tree outside the library that I had often admired for its glossy green leaves and sweet smell.

My journalling experience began in a predictable manner. I devoted an early page to recording the tree's scientific name and to describing its leaf forms and the texture and color of the bark. Each day, I sat in front of the tree and made the following entries: date, time, what the weather was like, and sightings of any insects or birds. By the third week of the semester, I was bored with the project, and had cut down my daily journal period to a five or ten minute stop on my way home from the library. The journal mirrored my boredom: its bland pages were densely filled with writing. The only visual variety was the occasional change in the color of the ink, from blue to black or brown.

One day my journalling took a surprising turn. While waiting to check out at the college bookstore, I spotted some wrapping paper that was the exact color of the newest leaves on my tree. The paper was glossy and delicate, just like the leaves. I bought it, and that night I cut out a piece of the luscious green paper and glued it to the next blank page of my journal. "This is the color of the leaves near the bottom" I wrote across the top of the page. The next day, I sat in front of the tree and sketched a leaf at the bottom of the green page.

A door in my imagination had swung open. The next day, I began drawing the pattern of the leaf

Grandpa brought his bread and love all the way from Sicily for me.

Joseph Osina uses this page of his journal to visually represent a memory of his grandfather. The colors, textures, and shapes evoke a particular state of mind far more effectively than a written description could.

Kerstin Vogdes sums up a day at the beach with loose, lively sketches and brief notes, and then includes an envelope of tiny shells and fragments which bring to life the colors, textures, and spirit of the beach.

veins, and noticed they were the same as the pattern of the tree's branches. Once I began noticing patterns, I saw more and more of them.

One day, I made rubbings of the tree's bark on tissue paper and glued them into the journal. I still noted the date, time, temperature, and weather, but designed small charts for this information and put the charts along the page margins.

I made lists and visual collections. One day I sketched every insect in the vicinity, then looked them up in an insect book and made a list of their scientific names and habitats. I drew details of the holes the insects made in the tree. I made a map of a trail of ants and discovered where they came from and where they were headed on the tree. I began looking at the tree as a habitat, the environment of insects and birds.

Some information was difficult to write about, so I found purely visual means of explaining it. I used a small set of watercolors to paint a color swatch of the feeling of each day. I huddled under the tree during a spring storm and painted the swaying movements of the tree in the wind.

As time passed, I became more and more curious about the tree. I inquired about its history, and found out it was in the way of a new path that was to be built that summer. I worried that the tree would be cut down and wrote its story on a piece of fragile tissue paper that I slipped into an envelope and glued inside the journal.

On the last day of the project, I went out to make my final journal entry. The book was now fat and splayed open, spilling its rich insides. I arrived at the library eager to record some final comments, only to find the tree gone, cut off a few inches above the ground. Sadly, I painted a black page that day, and glued some of the tree's sawdust around the edges.

My tree journal taught me that keeping a journal with both written and visual elements not only opens up new ways of composing pages, but new processes of thinking, feeling, observing, focusing, and experiencing life. If I had limited myself only to writing about the tree, I would never have been able to show what it felt like to be with the tree in a storm. I could never have expressed the beauty of the tree's patterns or the color of its leaves and bark. I would never have followed the ants or discovered the reason for their journey. I would not have known what to do with my feelings the day I discovered the tree cut down.

What can we call this deeper kind of journal with its richly-layered pages that integrate writing with visual elements? "Visual-verbal" comes close, but sounds a little dry and academic. "Annotated sketchbook" seems to place the value of the visual elements above the written part. Nature journalist Hannah Hinchman uses the term "the illuminated journal." Bruce Kremer, whose journal is shown on this page, calls it "the textured diary." In truth, this kind of journal is a marriage of form and content, of text or writing and visual expression. In this kind of journal, the way a page looks is determined by the thoughts and reflections expressed on the page. A certain idea or image will seem to need a certain kind of layout or design, and particular materials will allow you to express yourself more powerfully. Each element, visual and verbal, informs the other, and in turn informs your own understanding of the events, ideas, and reflections that you record. Painting in watercolors, for example, might make it easier to express feelings; using collage elements might help you recall an experience more vividly.

The great news is that creating beautiful, rich pages doesn't have to be time-consuming or difficult, even if you haven't touched paints since kindergarten. Just as the leafy green paper in the college bookstore opened my eyes to a new world of possibilities, the Materials section of this book will introduce you to a great variety of easy-to-use materials that can help you express your ideas and reflections in a deeper way. You'll learn how to conveniently store or

Bruce Kremer's complex arrangement of stamps, drawings, painting, typewritten text, and collage invites the viewer to meander around the page at a leisurely pace.

carry these materials so that they're accessible when you're ready to work on a page. We'll also look at setting up a practical work station for journalling and scrapbook-making activities.

Beginning with the Techniques section, we'll consider a range of readymade journals, sketchbooks, and albums, noting ways in which you can alter these books to better suit your own purposes. Removing pages, adding and changing elements, and embellishing covers can all add dimension and character to your book before you even begin to work on a page. You can save time and banish creative block by preparing your pages before you start to make journal entries. We'll explore several different processes that will give your pages a layered look, inspiring you to fill them with more creative forms of expression.

In the Layout section, you'll learn a number of different ways to compose the elements of a page in order to organize your thoughts in a certain way, as well as how to create a unified page that communicates your ideas effectively. You'll learn exactly how to get from a blank page to a rich page, brimming with meaning and delightful to look at.

The Applications section of the book explores several ways to jump-start the verbal or written aspect of journal keeping or scrapbook making, providing prompts for various kinds of entries that lend themselves to visual embellishment and integration with visual elements.

You'll see examples of 10 different types of page entries that will inspire you and help you organize your thoughts.

Throughout the book you'll find examples of various kinds of visual-verbal pages from different historical periods and cultures, and the pages were made for many purposes. These accompanying essays will help you place your own work within the context of this rich tradition.

Finally, the gallery examples throughout the book will introduce you to many beautiful and meaning-filled pages created by a variety of journal keepers. After you work through the book, these examples will be within reach, and they'll serve to inspire you to try different approaches to your own pages: you'll find yourself analyzing them, realizing that they were done using the same processes and materials that you've experimented with as you've worked with the ideas in this book.

Susan Saling's page communicates facts as well as the feeling of the Pere Lachaise cemetery in Paris. She combines her train ticket, parts of a cemetery brochure, her own sketch and painting, and a few written notes to summarize a day spent at this Paris attraction.

MATERIALS

Making art of any kind involves a series of choices that carries out your intentions for a particular piece of work. It's important to choose your materials and supplies as carefully as you choose the techniques you use or the thoughts and ideas you want to express in your journal.

Before you begin filling your blank book with your creative expressions, gather and organize your materials and supplies. This will help you leap over one of the biggest obstacles in journalling—lack of time. Naturally, if you have only a few minutes a day to devote to journalling, you won't want to spend that time hunting down supplies—you'll probably use only those materials that are readily at hand.

Let's say you want to paint a graceful violet and blue border to frame a journal entry about the wildflower walk you took this morning. Looking around, the only material you can find to work with is the crumb-covered red ballpoint pen you've fished out of the cushions of your chair. Your border is probably *not* going to happen. On the other hand, if you have art supplies, including a jar full of water, already laid out on the desk or in a box or on a nearby shelf, you can paint the mood-setting border in no more time than it would take to write about the colors of the day.

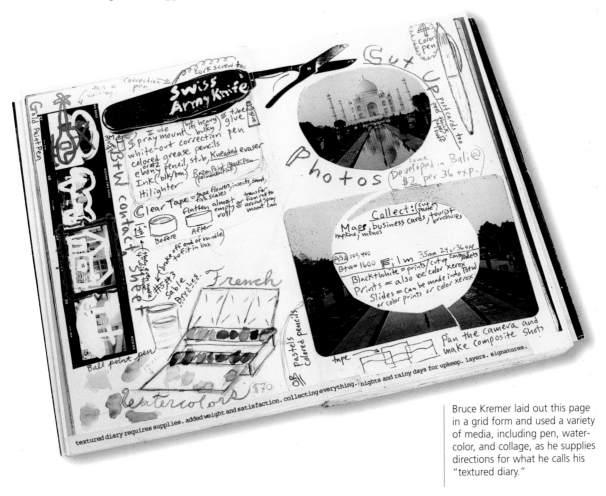

Bruce Kremer laid out this page in a grid form and used a variety of media, including pen, watercolor, and collage, as he supplies directions for what he calls his "textured diary."

The Basics

When you walk into an art or especially a craft supply store, you'll be confronted by a bewildering array of seductively beautiful, professionally designed papers, rubber stamps, ready-made stencils, and other materials that seem at first glance to be exactly what you need. But before deciding to buy these materials, keep in mind that they're already designed and already carry their own meaning. If you decide to use them, they'll require careful handling so their meaning doesn't dominate your work.

NEUTRAL OR DETERMINED MATERIALS

Art materials can be described as falling along a continuum from *neutral materials* (those that don't have any meaning or much connotation of their own) to *strongly determined materials* (those that carry meaning and connotations of their own). Neutral materials would include plain white sheets of paper, standard colors of paint, uncarved rubber stamp-making material, ordinary black ink, colored and graphite pencils, or any other materials that, rather than assert themselves, become transparent once they've been incorporated into artwork. Because these materials don't carry any meaning of their own, they won't interfere or conflict with the ideas that you're trying to express.

Strongly determined materials, at the other end of the continuum, already carry messages. There is a certain pale blue handmade paper, for example, that has delicate orange and yellow flowers embedded in it. It's very popular and instantly recognizable, which adds to its strength as a material. The papermaker's

Neutral materials can be easily shaped into any form of expression.

Strongly determined materials require careful use so that they don't dominate the work in which they're used.

choices—the color, texture, inlaid flowers—were just right for the original paper, but this paper, like anything often repeated, has become a cliché. The paper is so expressively strong that it tends to dominate and weaken any artwork in which it's used *unless* it's changed in some way or used very deliberately, relating to the content and concept of the piece.

Strongly determined materials like the pretty blue flower-inlaid paper require careful use. The collage in the photo (right) is a good example of successful use of strongly determined materials. The artist has cut and layered some easily-recognized popular papers to create a collage depicting a seashell. The whole is greater than the sum of the individual parts, and the parts lose their individual identities, disappearing into the design, just as they should.

When gathering materials, think about the meaning and connotation of the particular material, especially if it's strongly determined. Decide whether or not it can be used to express the ideas and feelings you want to get across in your work. If you decide to use some strongly determined materials, be sure that the meaning of the material contributes to the expression of your own meaning, and that it doesn't leap out and overwhelm your work. You can also use a strongly determined material ironically. For example, you might use excessively cute pre-carved rubber stamps of kittens and puppies to illustrate a book or journal entry about a serious subject: the population explosion of unwanted kittens and dogs, for instance.

ARCHIVAL QUALITY

Besides considering the meaning or neutrality of a material, there are a few other considerations to keep in mind when selecting blank books and other elements for your project. If you want the pages to last for a long time, buy materials that are acid-free or archival. Paper that's made from wood pulp is full of acid, and it will begin to deteriorate within a few months. Look for books made from acid-free or 100 percent cotton or rag paper. Some recycled paper is

Charlotte Hayes stitched a collage of strongly determined patterned papers into her book. PHOTO BY ELYSE WEINGARTEN

acid-free, but some isn't, so don't assume that recycled paper is the best paper to use. Since it's impossible to determine the acidity of a paper or cardboard just by looking at it, and many materials aren't labeled, consider buying a pH testing pen at an art supply store. This inexpensive pen is a good investment. It lets you make a small mark on the paper or cardboard that will turn one color if the paper is acidic and another color if it's neutral (see photo, below).

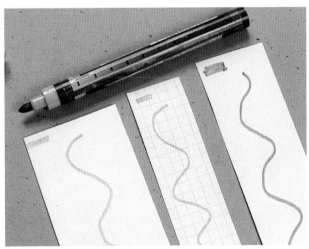

A pH testing pen will help you determine the acid content of your paper.

BLANK BOOKS

A blank book itself is a material, and as such it needs to be chosen and handled with the same careful consideration you use to choose other materials. Blank books, like other art materials, range from the neutral to the strongly determined. Neutral ones, such as the ones in the photo (below), are plain and unadorned and won't overwhelm your work. They can easily be made to blend with the expression of a wide variety of feelings and ideas. The insides and outsides of neutral blank books can be embellished, as described in Customizing a Blank Book (pages 34 to 40), or they can be left as they are—whatever suits your ideas for your particular project.

Blank books like those in the photo (opposite page, right) are more likely to intimidate you and find a permanent home on your bookshelf. These are the elegant, exquisitely made, hand-bound books that carry so much meaning of their own that they almost seem to challenge you to deface them with your paltry attempts at writing or drawing. Don't be frightened by them! Rather, consider carefully whether or not a particular book of this type will inhibit or enhance the feelings and ideas that you want to express in a specific project. A leather-bound book, for example, connotes traditional values of craftsmanship, elegance, and a certain formal restraint. It also offers good protection for the pages within, since leather is such a strong and durable material. This type of blank book might be the perfect book to use as a travel journal. Travel journals have a long tradition, making them very compatible with a traditional-looking book. Moreover, leather-bound books can withstand the heat of the sun, desert sand, seawater, dirt from a forest floor, as well as the stress of being pulled in and out of a pocket or pack many times.

A plain leather book might also be a great foil to a collection of riotously colored, very emotional pages that burst from within when the book is opened.

You can find these standard blank books at stationery, office supply, and gift stores, as well as art supply stores.

den or wildlife journal. But its earthy-looking cover could also form a nice contrast to an interior that deals with the memories of the process of building a house, an example of keeping nature at bay.

BINDING STYLES

A book's binding style is another important aspect to keep in mind. Sewn bindings last a great deal longer than glued bindings. Since you'll be opening and closing this book often, it must be able to withstand this frequent stress on the binding.

Traditional sewn bindings will stay open flat only if the pages are relatively large and made of a paper that drapes nicely rather than standing up stiffly when the book is opened. Closed-spine bindings afford good protection to pages and other elements incorporated into a book. Books with sewn bindings can be modified to prevent them from

Beautiful handmade books can be exactly what you need if you choose them to enhance your ideas.

The contrast between the restrained exterior and the unbridled interior can be exciting and full of meaning.

A blank book that has a cover decorated with natural materials would be an obvious good fit for a gar-

Blank books like this are suitable for nature journals, but may serve many other creative purposes.

A spiral binding is helpful if you want the pages to lie flat when the book is open, as in this journal by Ann Turkle.

FINDING YOUR SOUL CAN BE COMPLICATED.
GET THE MANUAL.

This is my soul manual
with floating clouds
undisturbed by jets streams
marring the sky alone
sheep grazing
with hope amongst the fabric
ivy leaves a trace
of years passing
soul fade ...

date unknown.

An album binding is a
good choice for Jennifer Wing's journal
with its numerous added elements and
heavily collaged pages.

splaying out if elements are glued onto pages (see
Adding and Changing Elements, pages 36 to 37).

Spiral or plastic comb bindings are relatively
durable and also allow a book to stay open flat—an
advantage if you'll be working in watercolor or other
wet media that must dry in an open position. The
natural springiness of these bindings allows elements
to be added to pages. You can glue additions onto
many pages and the book will still close flat, not
splay out as a tighter binding would. These bindings,
however, don't afford as much protection to pages as
closed-spine bindings.

Books that are sewn in the Japanese stab-binding
manner (see photo, left) are durable, but don't stay
open very well by themselves.

Album bindings (see photo, above) are strong and
usually have some spine thickening modifications so
they don't splay out when you glue elements to
pages. You can unbind and re-bind these bindings
easily so pages can be removed or added. These
books do not generally stay open flat unless the
pages are large and heavy enough to drape.

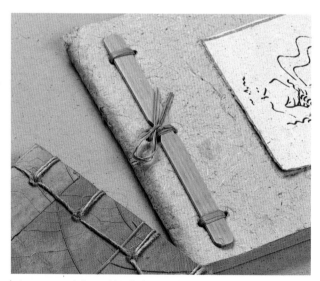

Japanese stab-bound books have a distinctive look.

Right: Blank books come in a variety of paper types.

PAPER

The thickness and finish of the paper in a book should figure into your decisions. Very thin, lightweight paper won't accept wet media such as acrylic paint or watercolors without wrinkling and possibly tearing. Some inks and stamp pad dyes will bleed through onto the verso, or backside, of these thin pages. Thin papers can also be problematic if you want to attach items to the pages. Ideally, your paper and the elements you add to it should be equally heavy. Thin papers can work well if, for example, you want to emphasize the delicacy of the wildflowers you plan to draw with colored pencils in a nature journal. Just be aware of the limitations of thin paper, and consider the media you use in relation to the weight of the paper.

If you plan to do a lot of painting in your blank book, you may want to use a book made with watercolor paper pages. However, if you want pages that drape nicely and feel soft, this rather stiff paper might not be appropriate. Adding some sheets of watercolor paper to a book that has moderately heavy, more graceful pages could be a better solution (see pages 36 to 37).

You will learn by experience what kinds of paper work best with the media you prefer. The way paper receives liquid media depends on whether or not it contains *sizing*. Sizing is a kind of glue added to paper to stop it from absorbing water. Sizing allows you to write on paper with liquid ink. Most blank books have sized paper, but if you buy one made with unsized paper, you'll need to write with a ballpoint pen or a pencil instead of a liquid ink pen. In general, very smooth, hard-finished paper is not as receptive to drawing media as softer, rougher (or *toothier*) paper. Hard, smooth paper isn't very absorbent, and inks from media such as pigment-based stamp pads won't dry on it quickly.

Art Supplies

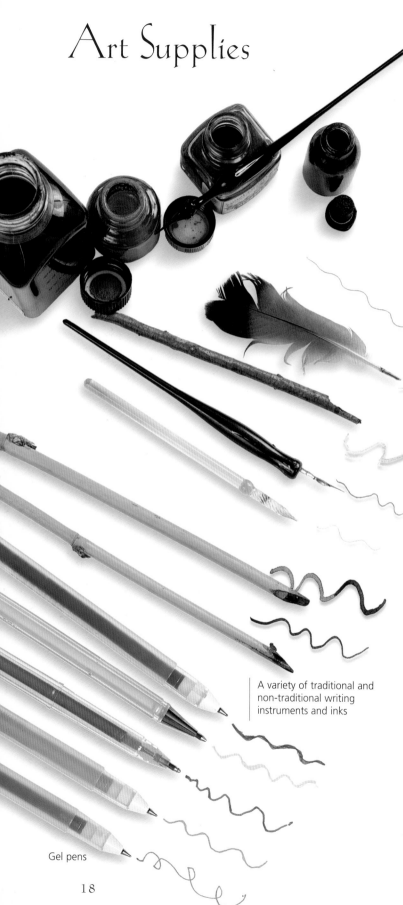

A variety of traditional and non-traditional writing instruments and inks

Gel pens

Moving from a blank page to a page rich in texture and expression requires not only your unbridled creativity, but some advanced planning. Start by assembling a collection of art supplies—everything from basic pens to the scraps and ephemera of your life. These will become the building blocks you'll use to record your experiences and reflections. Different materials will help create different moods or tones for your pages, and through experimentation, you'll be able to choose just the right materials to express your feeling accurately.

The materials in this section were chosen because they dry completely and don't rub off onto facing pages. In adding visual and verbal elements to books, it's crucial to use media that don't smear or rub off when pages meet. These are also materials that won't bleed through most paper surfaces. Finally, these media are, for the most part, acid-free or archival and won't degrade the book paper over time. As you experiment and discover new media to use in books, always ask these questions about new materials: Do they result in a stable surface that won't rub off or smear? Do they bleed through? Are they acid-free or archival?

PENS AND INKS

Pen and ink is a basic medium for writing in journals and blank books. The range of available pens and inks is enormous, and rather than try to describe what is best learned by experience, I will present some categories of pens and inks and encourage you to find out for yourself which feel best and make the kind of marks you want to make.

BASIC BLACK EXTRA-FINE STEEL OR PLASTIC-TIP WATERPROOF PENS

Most steel or plastic-tip waterproof pens are inexpensive, last a long time, and reliably make fine, dense black lines. They're indispensable for writing as well as for quick sketches. They're capable of producing a variety of textures and tones and can be used very successfully in careful drawing. Some brands also come in brown (sepia), blue, red, purple, and green; but often colored inks are not waterproof.

GEL PENS

Similar to ballpoint pens, but filled with opaque pastel or metallic ink, gel pens work especially well on dark papers. Most have fine tips, and many have inks that are acid-free or archival (unlike conventional ballpoint pens, which are not recommended for journaling because they're very acidic and never completely dry).

METALLIC PENS

Metallic pens come in various tip widths. The most effective ones are gold, silver, or bronze pens, and are solvent based. Shake them for a few minutes before using them. Some of these pens stain paper if they're incompletely mixed. Many blot at the beginning of a line, so it's important to keep scratch paper handy when using these pens.

DIP PENS AND INKS

You can draw or write with sticks, twigs, feathers, coffee stirrers, and many other objects in addition to metal nibs in pen holders. Experiment with Italian glass pens, thin-line crow quill pens, or hand-carved bamboo reed pens. Make pens out of sticks and reeds that you find at hand while you're making a journal entry. When you discover which instruments work best for you, experiment some more until you find the perfect ink. Art supply stores sell vibrant, transparent, varnish-based inks in glowing colors, luminous pearlescent inks, crackling metallics, as well as jet black and smoky gray.

SPECIALTY INKS

If you research carefully, you can find inks made of walnuts, wine, and oak galls. You can also make your own inks from strong coffee, teas, and beet juice.

Metallic pens (and metallic stamp pad ink) draw the eye to the text in spite of the strongly textured border of this page by Nina Bagley.

Brown ink gives this page by Dusty Benedict a soft look.

GRAPHITE PENCILS

Like pens, graphite pencils are basic pieces of equipment. Art supply stores sell these in a range of hardness, which is determined by the ratio of graphite to binder. "B" pencils are softer pencils—the higher the number before the B, the softer the pencil. Softer pencils have less waxy binder, and, therefore, make darker marks and are easier to smear. Harder pencils are called "H" pencils—the higher the number, the harder the pencil. Since you need to avoid a smeary, fragile surface, stay away from extremely soft pencils. A good range is between 3B and 2H. Keep a pencil pointer and sandpaper handy to sharpen your pencils.

Some graphite pencils are made with a water-soluble binder, and these can be made into a watercolor-like wash by brushing the pencil strokes with water. Even regular graphite pencil lines can be turned into washes by using mineral spirits and a brush.

White colored pencil makes an effective contrast to a graphite sketch on blue paper on this page by Susan Saling.

COLORED PENCILS

Colored pencils come in two basic families: water soluble and non-water soluble. Water-soluble pencils tend to be lower in intensity or brightness than non-water-soluable ones. They can be used for writing and drawing and can also be stroked onto a page to create layers of color. These layers can then be turned into washes by brushing them with a wet brush, or more color can be stroked on, and textures and stroke marks can be left on top of the washes.

Non-water-soluble or waxy colored pencils tend to be more vibrant and intense than the water-soluble ones. They're somewhat transparent so they can be layered to produce an infinite number of subtle mixes. Contrary to what many technical manuals state, colored pencils can be lightened and even erased. To do so, make a small masking tape loop, leaving the sticky side of the tape facing outward. Wrap the loop around your finger, then tap the colored pencil marks with the sticky side of the tape loop. Depending on how long you tap, you can significantly lighten and even completely remove colored pencil marks from most papers this way without damaging the surface of the paper.

Waxy colored pencil markings can be turned into washes by using mineral spirits and a brush over colored areas.

CRAYONS

In addition to basic wax crayons, art supply stores also sell water-soluble crayons. Both kinds are useful for adding visual elements to a page. Regular wax crayons can be used in the process of wax resist, in which a light-colored crayon is used to draw a shape

Wax crayons

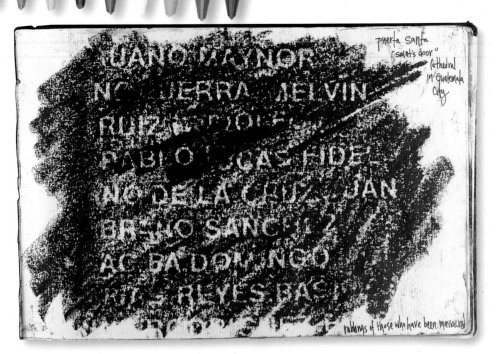

puerta santa
"saint's door"
(athedral
in Guatemala
City

rubbings of those who have been massacred

The roughness of a wax crayon rubbing helps this page by Colleen Stanton shout its message.
PHOTO BY ELYSE WEINGARTEN

or shapes. Watercolor washes are then brushed over the shape and its background. The watercolor adheres only to the non-waxy areas of the paper, yielding an interesting surface that can look something like batik.

Water-soluble crayons work just like water-soluble colored pencils but they have thicker points. They also deposit a heavier layer of pigment onto the paper, and when they are brushed over with water, the resulting surface is somewhat grainy, which adds an interesting texture.

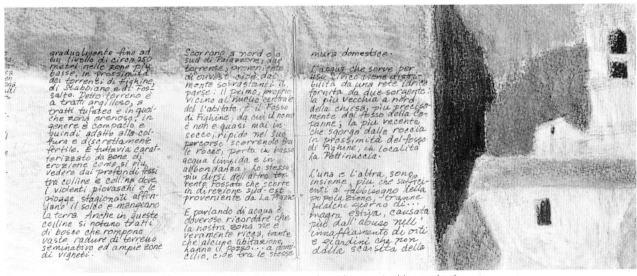

Watercolor crayons can be turned into a wash by brushing over marks with water. In this page by the author, some texture was drawn back into the wash after it was dry. PHOTO BY ELYSE WEINGARTEN

PAINTS

The best paints for bookwork are watercolors and gouache (opaque watercolors). Both are water-based, and both dry completely, with no surface stickiness. Watercolors are transparent to semi-transparent, whereas gouache is opaque to semi-opaque. Even if you're mainly interested in using watercolors, a tube of white gouache would be a good addition to your watercolor palette. White gouache mixes with watercolor to make pastels that can add nice contrast to watercolors. White gouache by itself is useful for adding highlights to watercolor sketches.

Gouache is more opaque than watercolor and is capable of giving very bright colors, as in this page by Kelcey Loomer. PHOTO BY ELYSE WEINGARTEN

items—tickets, receipts, notes, napkin sketches, wrapping paper, scraps of handwriting, sugar packets, seed packages, labels, magazine and newspaper clippings, pressed flowers, stamps, paper bags, and fortune cookie fortunes—use them as the bases of designs, in patterns, and as the starting point of drawings. Attach them to your pages with acid-free tape or adhesive. If a particular surface won't take dry adhesive, use a glue stick or a drop of PVA. Keep in mind that heavily collaged pages fatten the fore edge of a book. You'll need

COLLAGE

At the heart of many journals and scrapbooks are the scraps—the ephemera of a journey, an experience, a project, or daily life. Collect these flat

Christine Toriello used train tickets as a base for this ink, color, and watercolor page. Its grid nicely echoes the repetition of the train cars. PHOTO BY ELYSE WEINGARTEN

A letter stencil was used to render clean crisp letters on this page by the author. The tiles in the grid design are an example of wax crayon resist.
PHOTO BY ELYSE WEINGARTEN

Stencils come in a variety of sizes and lettering styles.

to compensate for this extra bulk by removing a page or two immediately in front of the collage (see pages 35 to 37).

If some original items are too bulky to attach to the book itself, make color photocopies of them at a copy center, and attach (or transfer) them to the journal. Pressed leaves and flower petals can be preserved and protected by brushing them with matte or satin finish polymer varnish. Varnish will glue the flattened organic material to the page and also seal out air and moisture.

STENCILS

Lettering is an important design element, and you can broaden the range of lettering on your pages by using various lettering guides or stencils. You can find these at craft, drafting, or office supply stores. Choose different fonts or letter styles so you'll have ones that suit various moods or purposes. You can also use the stencil for the basic letter shape, then embellish the letters to tailor them to the project at hand.

STAMPS OR RELIEF PRINTS

In a relief print, the design area is raised above a flat surface so that the raised area prints and the recessed background doesn't. A fingerprint is a simple example of a relief print: the ink attaches itself to the raised ridges of our fingers—the print reflects only the ridges and not the "valleys" in between.

You can make your own small relief printing blocks, or stamps, out of rubber or plastic erasers, corks, or even foam earplugs. You might try carving an alphabet or numerals and make stamps of motifs or designs from the environment about which you are writing and drawing.

To carve a stamp, draw a shape onto a cork or eraser with black pen. Remember that the image will print in reverse of the stamp, so be sure to draw letters and numerals in reverse. Use linoleum carving tools or a razor knife to cut away the background, leaving the design area raised (in relief). Corks may need to be lightly sanded before carving or have a thin slice removed from their sometimes bumpy ends.

Keep in mind, however, that your image will be in reverse when you print, so if you're carving letters, you'll need to carve them backwards to get the right orientation when you print. If you're using rubber eraser material, you can draw a design or letter on paper with a graphite pencil, then transfer the image by simply rubbing it on to the carving material, and then carve it.

Craft knives and linoleum carving tools are effective for carving stamps.

Graphite transfers onto rubber eraser material easily.

You can easily buy commercial rubber stamps at craft supply stores, but be sure to use these materials with care so that they don't dominate your work (see section on Neutral and Determined Materials, pages 12 to 13).

Buy stamp pads from craft supply stores, keeping in mind that dye-based inks dry faster than pigment-style inks, but pigment-style inks tend to be more opaque and more intense in color. Dye-based inks also bleed through some papers.

Stamp prints can be used alone, in borders, and even to design entire backgrounds or page surfaces.

The swallows on this page were created by using a handcarved cork stamp.

STITCHING

A sometimes overlooked way of making marks is stitching. Stitched lines lend color and texture to a page. A stitched border is a tactile as well as a visual element.

You can stitch on paper with an ordinary needle and thread. Just be sure to tighten the thread by pulling parallel to the surface of the page. If you keep your hand or fingers in contact with the page as you gently pull, you won't tear the paper. You can also use a sewing machine to stitch pages. Experiment with the tension and stitch length to get a good flat stitch.

Depending on the expressive content of your page, you might consider using brightly colored silk threads, glittering metallics, or stark, crisp black.

Stitching can also be used very effectively to attach collage elements to a page and also to attach fold outs, small booklets, and envelopes to page stubs.

The author stitched a border onto this page to frame the central ink sketch. PHOTO BY ELYSE WEINGARTEN

Everyday Supply Kit

All the page preparation materials you'll use everyday can be kept in one small box.

– Small jar (with a screw-on lid) full of clean water
– Small watercolor set, either tubes or pans, including the basic colors: alizarin crimson, pthalo or ultramarine blue, gamboge yellow, yellow ochre, raw sienna, pthalo green, Payne's gray*
– #12 round watercolor brush**
– Mixing tray (old pie tin or an inexpensive watercolor mixing pan)
– Scissors
– Small set of watercolor pencils
– Small set of water-soluble pastel crayons
– Plain lettering guide (stencil)***
– Rubber stamp letters, commercial or handcarved
– Rubber stamp carving material, corks, erasers
– Linoleum carving tool set
– Dye-based and pigment-based stamp pads, black and multicolored
– Small box of regular wax crayons
– Pens and inks (black, colored, metallics, but preferably not ballpoint pens with acidic ink)
– Waterproof black fine-line pen
– Graphite pencils and erasers
– Small container of citrus-based gel-type paint stripper for solvent transfers
– Collage items— labels, stamps, old letters, wrapping papers, magazine images, other memorabilia and ephemera from your life
– Color and black-and-white photocopies for transfers (photos, maps, etc.)

– Flat, soft 1-inch (2.5 cm) wide brush
– Rag
– PVA or acid-free, permanent roll-on adhesive
– Glue brush (if using PVA)
– White gouache (opaque watercolor, either a tube or a jar)
– Small self-healing cutting mat

*You can add other colors if you want to, but these will get you started. Also, don't worry if the set you buy doesn't have exactly these colors. Just get a basic set.
**This is a good starter brush. Add others as you need them.
***Choose one sized to fit the pages you're working on.

27

Supply Kit for Customizing Books and Preparing Pages

- Stencil brush
- Matte knife or craft knife
- Masking tape
- Fluid or liquid acrylics*
- Small empty liquid detergent bottle or other squeeze bottles or medicine droppers
- Sponge with flat sides
- Blotter paper
- Old newspaper
- Plastic needlepoint canvas, #7 or bigger holes
- Thin metal sheets, paper, or cloth with patterns of holes cut out of them
- Decorative edge scissors, one or two pairs
- Envelopes for gluing into journal
- Tracing paper
- Graph paper or other kinds of drawing or writing paper
- Watercolor paper or set of blank watercolor postcards or note cards
- Small ruler, 12 inches long (30.5 cm) or shorter

- Cotton make-up removal pads
- Cling-style plastic wrap
- Table salt in a shaker
- Acrylic matte medium
- Polymer varnish (either satin, matte, or gloss finish)
- Sand, seeds, talcum powder, shells, etc. (for encrustation)
- Scraps of mat board or other lightweight cardboard

*Get small bottles in several colors. Be sure to include some metallics if you like their look.

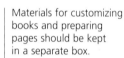

Materials for customizing books and preparing pages should be kept in a separate box.

28

SETTING UP A WORKSTATION

Once you've assembled all your supplies, find two boxes to keep them in. If you're going to keep your everyday supplies out on a desk or table, the box doesn't need to have a lid. Keep the water jar full of clean water, ready for action. Refill it after using it and put the lid on it, and it'll always be ready. You'll be surprised at how much more often you'll use watercolors if you don't have to get up first to fill the jar with water! If you don't have a permanent workplace, get a box with a lid and store it on a convenient shelf, under a bed, or in a centrally located closet.

Keep the supplies for customizing books and preparing pages in a separate, lidded box, as you won't use these as often as the everyday supplies.

TRAVEL SUPPLY KIT

If you're going to work on your book outside or away from your house, you'll need to streamline your supplies and keep the ones you use on a daily basis in a small travel case, such as the one shown. Select your favorite supplies, perhaps buying smaller than usual sizes of some items. Even a traveling supply kit—if it includes watercolors—needs a plastic jar full of water; a small shampoo bottle and the outer lid from a can of shaving cream work very well.

Keep some supplies in a travel kit for spontaneous journal entries away from home.

Illogical Illuminations

From inside its glass museum case, the page glows with life. The hand-written text, beautifully lettered and embellished with graceful flourishes and ornate initials, surrounds a tranquil scene of praying women. Gold illuminates the halos around their bowed heads. The tendrils of vines form an intricate border that gently leads the eye to the margins of the page. But there the serious religious mood is abruptly shattered. The margins are the site of romping monsters, a monkey riding backwards on a donkey, a hooded person glancing skeptically at the text, and a hedgehog munching on the vines themselves. The margins seem to poke fun at the central part of the page, yet they are drawn with as much care as the central illustration. What is going on here?

The book is an illuminated manuscript, one of many that were made from the sixth through the mid-15th centuries in Europe. Created before the invention of printing, these books were hand-copied and hand-painted, mostly by monastic scribes. In later years, such books were made by artisans working on commission. Technically, the word "illumination" refers to the gold and silver that were used on most of these books to bring light into the manuscripts.

Illuminated manuscripts were produced throughout Europe by diverse groups of scribes and artisans over a long period of time. All of them have a few things in common. They were all done on prepared animal skins (parchment) at first and later hand-made rag paper. Most of the earlier manuscripts have religious subject matter. The production of these books involved different people doing different parts of the job. Often, several scribes copied different parts of an original onto prepared parchment. Usually someone else compared the copies to the original and made corrections in the margins. Finally, an artist or artists embellished the manu-

"Saint Bartholomew Apostle," from *The Book of Hours of Catherine of Cleves*, Netherlands (Utrecht), c. 1435.
COURTESY OF THE PIERPONT MORGAN LIBRARY/ART RESOURCE NY

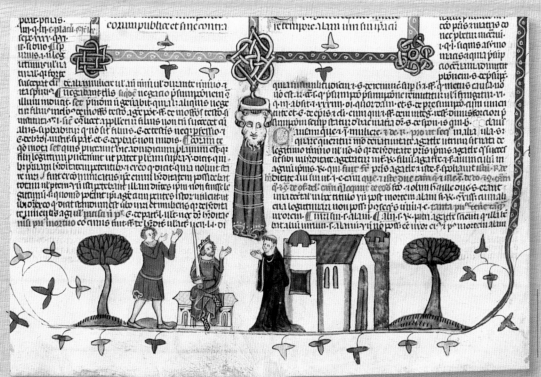

script by adding initials, chapter headings, illustrations, and marginal drawings. Often, several artists worked on the same page at different times. One might draw a cartoon or sketch, another would lay gold or silver leaf onto areas that were to be illuminated, and still another would paint in colors, sometimes following directions given by the sketcher. Finally, a binder gathered the sheets and sewed the book together.

The presence of several artisans working on the same page may account for the strange things that happen on some pages. There are, of course, many manuscript pages featuring mostly text with a few simple flourishes (perhaps in a second color) on the initials and a plain ruled border. There are also many pages on which text and a central illustration support one another and tell the same story. But there are some pages in which, while text and central illustration support one another, the illustrations in the margins tell a totally contradictory story. The margins of some pages are filled with monkeys, acrobats, monsters, jugglers, thieves, knights and ladies, nuns and monks, all in a variety of often bawdy scenes.

Occasionally, a margin figure points at a line of text and makes a face, showing disagreement. In one page from *The Book of Hours of Catherine of Cleves,* the sober figure of St. Bartholomew the apostle is the central image, but the margins are lined with a border of pretzels and biscuits. Hooded men and monks sit in each corner of the page, tugging on the pretzel twists, as if trying to keep the page together (see photo above).

On some illuminated pages, blank spaces after a line of text are filled with the elongated bodies of monsters, some of which communicate with each other and with the marginal figures (who are busily going about acting out a scene that has nothing to do with the text). The activities in the margins often deal with subject matter that was marginalized by society, pushed from the center of daily life, or even pushed to the edges of general awareness.

In later manuscripts, a different kind of play between text and various images began to happen. In northern Europe in the 15th century, a new kind of margin begins to take the place of cavorting monkeys and monsters. On these pages the margins are filled with extremely realistic *trompe l'oeil* (literally "fool the eye") objects from everyday life. The margins become three-dimensional architectural elements, cupboard-like structures framing the deep space of the miniature painting and the text. Three systems of seeing collide on these pages. The viewer's eye travels between the deep space of the miniature scene (which was supposed to enhance meditation on the prayer contained in the text), the flatness of the text, and the objects in the margins, which seem to project forward and beg to be lifted from the page. These realistic margins create a distraction from the main business of the page, while the careful perspective drawing of the miniature exerts a pull back to prayer.

It is only possible to touch on the complicated subject of medieval page design here. For a thorough discussion and a wealth of examples, see Michael Camille's book *Images on the Edge: The Margins of Medieval Art* (1992, Harvard University Press).

Techniques

Now that your supplies are assembled, you've got almost everything you need to start transforming your blank book into a creative, expressive journal or album. One thing you may still need is more time to work on it! In this section of the book, you'll learn to prepare your book and pages in advance so you're ready to start working on your entries when the creative spirit moves you. We'll explore techniques for adapting your book, preparing pages in advance, and laying the groundwork for what will become a richly-layered book. First, we'll look at customizing a blank book. You'll discover ways to adapt your book to accommodate the elements you may want to add, giving you more flexibility to go beyond the confines of a traditional book format. Next, we'll explore techniques for modifying a cover, helping you to create an appealing and inviting book that you'll want to return to again and again. Finally, we'll learn several page preparation techniques that you can use to start creating richer pages in advance, so that when you're ready to begin using a page, you'll start out with a beautifully-laid foundation.

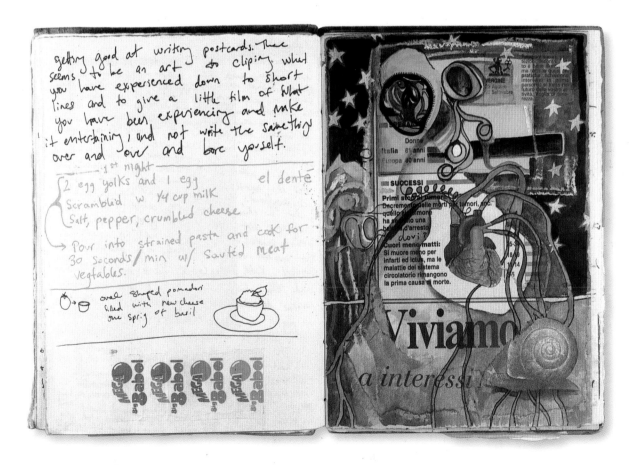

Kelcey Loomer, *Untitled Journal Page*, 2000. PHOTO BY ELYSE WEINGARTEN

Customizing a Blank Book

Customizing a book is a relatively nonthreatening way to begin to interact with it. Let's assume you've already chosen a blank book to use for a journal or scrapbook. It might be one that you went out and bought specifically for a project, or it might be one that has been living on your bookshelf for a while. In either case, it may need a little customizing to make it the perfect vehicle for the kinds of pages you intend to create, the kinds of ideas and feelings you want to express, or the job you want your journal to do. Following are some easy-to-make changes. Please note that it's perfectly fine to make no changes at all. It's equally fine to make every one of the suggested changes. The guiding principle is the idea and/or feeling that you want to express in your book. Only you can decide whether and how to modify your book.

Pamela Lyle Westhaver, *Salt Spring 2000*, 2000. Assorted papers, memorabilia, surface decorations, watercolor pencils, pencil, and crayon. PHOTO BY ARTIST

REMOVING PAGES

If you want to add elements such as collage to the pages in your book, you'll need to modify the book because extra materials tend to make it bulk up and splay open. There's a secret to keeping a book from bulging open when you add in elements: equalize the thickness of the spine with the thickness of the fore edge of the book. There's nothing you can do to increase the thickness of the spine of a sewn or glued book, but you can reduce the thickness of the fore edge so that added elements simply plump it back to its original size. To do this, you will need to remove some pages. A rule of thumb is to remove one or two pages (depending on the thickness of the paper) before every page on which you intend to glue a collage element, photograph, or any other added item. This is assuming that the added items are flat and of the approximate thickness of the removed page or pages.

You Will Need

– Cutting mat
– Ruler
– Craft knife

Instructions

Place a small, thin cutting mat under the page to be removed, pushing it back toward the spine as far as it will easily go. Use a ruler and craft knife to cut the page away approximately ½ inch (1.3 cm) in from the spine edge.

For a particular expressive reason, you might prefer to cut a wavy line or some irregular line instead of using a ruler. The resulting page stub can also become a design element if you color it, draw on it, write on it, paint on it, etc.

ADDING SPINE FATTENERS TO ALBUMS

Most blank albums come with spine fatteners or stubs (pieces of paper the height of the text pages, but only as wide as the spine part of the pages). If yours doesn't have them and you plan to glue elements to the pages, open the binding by either untying it or unscrewing the metal posts, and insert spine fatteners.

You Will Need
– Heavy paper
– Scissors
– Hole Punch

Instructions

1 Cut spine fatteners from heavy paper. They need to be the width of the spine portion of the cover and the height of the pages of the album.

2 Punch or drill holes in the spine fatteners in exactly the same place as holes in the pages, relative to the spine edge.

3 Interleaf each page with a spine fattener, and then re-bind the album.

ADDING AND CHANGING ELEMENTS

You might decide that you would like to add elements to your book: an envelope for collecting seeds, some sheets of watercolor paper, colored paper, tracing paper, or beautiful wrapping paper from that small shop in the village you visited last weekend. The following is good method for adding to your blank book:

You Will Need
– Cutting mat
– Craft knife
– PVA or other adhesive

Instructions

1 Begin by removing one page (or two, depending on the thickness of the paper you will add), as directed in the instructions on page 35.

2. Run a bead of PVA or roll-on adhesive along the spine edge of the element you want to add, and press it to the front of the page stub.

3. If you've cut off two pages, put glue on the front of the second stub, and lay the additional element on it. Run another bead of PVA along the back of the first page stub and press it on top of the spine edge of the add-on element.

Variation

Another way to attach elements to a page is by using eyelets and an eyelet plier, available in fabric stores (see photo, below). Follow the directions given with the eyelet pliers to join elements together.

Above: Nina Bagley uses small metal eyelets to attach pages to page stubs and to add elements to pages.

LAMINATING A PAGE

You can laminate (completely glue) one page on top of another page in a book. If the paper that you want to laminate is on the heavy or moderately heavy side, begin by removing the page or pages before the one to which you'll laminate (see directions for removing a page, on page 35).

You Will Need
– Paper
– Scissors or craft knife
– PVA or roll-on adhesive

Instructions

1 Cut the paper that you want to laminate so that it's the same size as the page to which it will be laminated, minus a vertical strip along the spine edge equal to the preceding page stub.

2 Spread PVA or roll-on adhesive over the back of the element to be laminated. Line up the element with the fore edge and the base page, and press the pages together (see photo, below left).

3 Slip a piece of wax paper into the book on top of and below the laminated page, and close the book to press the pages while they dry.

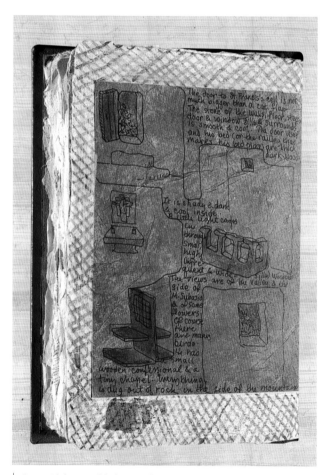

Gwen Diehn, *Untitled Journal Page*, 2001. PHOTO BY ELYSE WEINGARTEN

Tab Dividers

If your book is going to have different sections that you will want to locate quickly, consider laminating a tabbed divider page at the beginning of each section.

You Will Need
– Matte knife or craft knife
– Cutting mat
– PVA
– Heavy Paper

Instructions
Laminate your page so that the tab extends ¼ inch (6 mm) or so beyond the text block, or pages, of the book (see photo, below).

Variation
You can also use found objects or collage as tabs. Just make sure that they are securely fastened to your page and will stand up to wear and tear (see photo, below).

Above: Nina Bagley uses found objects attached with eyelets as tab dividers.

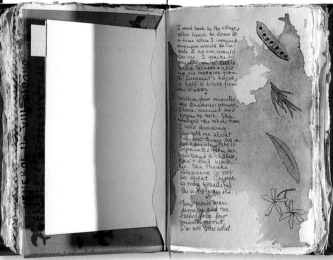

Right: Gwen Diehn, *Untitled Journal Page*, 2001. The page to the left has a tab sheet laminated to it. PHOTO BY ELYSE WEINGARTEN

EDGE TRIMMING

Another way to change the appearance of a book is to modify the edges of the pages.

You Will Need
– Sharp-edged metal ruler
– Cutting mat
– Decorative edge scissors

Instructions

1 Slip a cutting mat under two or three pages at a time, then use a sharp-edged metal ruler to hold the pages down while you tear a narrow (about ¼ inch {6 mm}) strip from the edges of each page. Depending on the thickness of the paper, you may be able to tear two or even three pages at once.

2 For a crisper look, use decorative edge scissors to cut the edges of the pages. If your book has a soft cover, you can even cut the edges of the covers this way (see photos, right and below).

Above: Coral Jensen used decorative edge scissors to give a richly textured look to the text block of this journal.

ALTERED BOOKS

One of the strongest presences in the film "The English Patient" is not a person but the journal that the leading character carries everywhere. The journal is first seen before the story even begins, when one of its pages is used as the backdrop against which the beginning credits roll. The paper is slightly textured and warm terra-cotta in tone, and a paintbrush held by an unseen person is painting abstract swimming or dancing figures on it. Later in the film, there is a scene that explains this initial image: one of the characters sits in a cave and paints figures that have been discovered on the cave walls onto a piece of paper. She later gives the sketches to the journal-keeper, who pastes them into his journal.

The journal appears in so many scenes throughout the movie that it becomes a thread that holds together the many shifting locations and flashbacks of the story. In the novel on which the film is based, author Michael Ondjaanti introduces the journal in this way:

> She picks up the notebook that lies on the small table beside his bed. It is the book he brought with him through the fire—a copy of the *Histories* by Herodotus that he has added to, cutting and gluing in pages from other books or writing in his own observations—so that all are cradled within the text of Herodotus.

> (*The English Patient*, Knopf, 1992, page 16)

The leading character, who is named Almasy, calls the journal his "commonplace book," and it is his constant companion. It's no ordinary journal, but rather a journal grafted onto his favorite book. Almasy's journal entries are a mixture of text and visuals—sketches, maps, a few old photographs, and memorabilia, most of which have been written on and then glued in. In some scenes in the movie, Almasy pastes sketches into his journal, while in other scenes he writes around the margins of the pages and on the empty pages at the front and back of the text. In a number of scenes, he reads (or is read to) from Herodotus's text. In a few close up shots, it's possible to see that the journal is rich and many-layered. Almasy values it above all his other possessions.

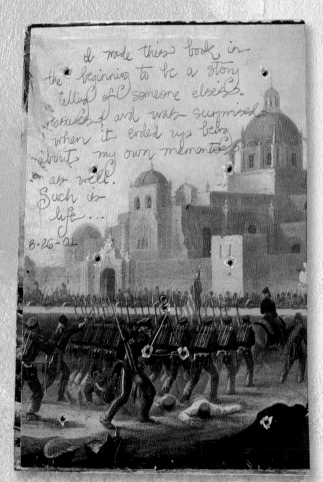

Nina Bagley, *Inside Cover of Altered Book*, 2000.

Almasy's journal is what book artists call an *altered book*. Using a found book and then altering it adds a dimension to journaling that can greatly enrich the experience. If the original book is one that has strong meaning for the journaler, the book becomes a foil against which the journal entries are played. The journaler might expand, contrast, question, endorse, or argue with the original text. The marginal entries can become a gloss, or commentary, on the text, in the manner of comments written in the margins of medieval manuscripts (see pages 30 to 32). Another approach to altered books is to indirectly respond to the original book by using it simply as a mood-setting background. A travel journal might be made out of an old atlas, for example.

One way to proceed with a found book is to paint out much of the text with white gouache before writing in it. It could be interesting to leave selected words or phrases and incorporate them into journal entries. Another idea is to cut away parts of pages to expose selected passages further back in the book and incorporate these passages into multiple new entries. It's always possible to paste different paper over whole or partial pages, and write and draw on the pasted-on paper. Some journalers use only the original covers, carefully rebinding blank pages inside them.

Whichever approach you use, converting a found structure into a journal can change your journal-keeping significantly. It can be a way of incorporat-

Jenny Taliadoros, *Evolution*, altered book from The World and Man, © University of Chicago, 1937. Collage and painting. PHOTO BY ARTIST

ing a beloved book from childhood into your daily life; or of keeping the words of another writer before you as you go about recording and interweaving your own thoughts and experiences. It can allow you to carry on a kind of conversation with another writer or furnish delicious opportunities for irony and play-ful commentary.

Of course, using an existing book nicely solves the problem of facing a blank page. Preparing pages in such a book involves choosing what to keep, what to modify, and what to obliterate from the original. Another benefit of using such a book is that many old bindings are elegant as well as durable. An after-noon spent in a used bookstore can yield leather-bound books with marbled endpapers and gilded fore edges, all for a fraction of the cost of a new blank book of comparable quality. Old photo albums, atlases, anatomy textbooks, encyclopedias, children's books, dictionaries, and books in foreign languages are just a sampling of the many possibilities that await the found book journal-keeper.

Above: Jenny Taliadoros, *The Wine and the Music*, altered book from The Wine and the Music.
©DOUBLEDAY AND CO, 1968. PHOTO BY ARTIST

Karen Michel, *Art Journal 2001* (Inside spread), 2001. Gesso, acrylic medium, collage. PHOTO BY ARTIST

Modifying the Cover

Besides changing the pages in a book, you can also customize the cover. The changes you make can range from simply drawing or painting a title on the cover to completely changing its texture and appearance. You can make changes to a cover before or after you start working on the inside of the book.

Coral Jensen, *Untitled Journal Cover*, 2000.

ENCRUSTATION

A hardcover book can be completely transformed by a process called *encrustation* which was developed by book artist Timothy Ely. The effects that you can achieve with this process are limited only by your imagination.

You Will Need
- Acrylic matte medium
- 1 quart (.95 L) jar for mixing
- Thickener or texturizing material*
- Masking tape
- Small squares of cardboard or matboard
- PVA glue
- Dinner knife, palette knife, or putty knife (optional)
- Old credit cards (optional)
- Embedding materials, such as small scraps of cardboard and leather, twigs, mica, shells, cloth, etc.
- Sandpaper (optional)
- Nails (optional)
- Carving tools (optional)
- Liquid acrylic paints
- Shoe polish (optional)
- Paste wax (optional)
- Rags

*You can use whiting powder (calcium carbonate, available from art supply stores that sell printmaking materials) or talc for a smooth texture; sand for a rougher texture; and small seashells, pebbles, or seeds for an uneven texture.

Instructions

1 Pour about 1 inch (2.5 cm) of matte medium into the jar. Add whiting (calcium carbonate) or talc powder to make a thick paste. Stir to mix completely.

2 Because encrustation doesn't work well on hinges or folds, cover the spine and hinge of each cover with masking tape before proceeding. If you want a design that is raised above the surface of the book, glue on pieces of cardboard or leather to form these relief areas.

3 Trowel the encrusting material onto one cover of the book, spreading it as you go. Cover the entire surface except for any areas that are masked off. If you want a particularly thick encrustation, it's better to do it in several layers, letting each layer dry completely before going on to each subsequent one (see photo, below).

4 Embed pieces of mica, cloth, rocks, beads, etc., by pushing or pressing them into the encrustation.

5 Let the encrustation dry. This may take several hours, depending on the thickness of the encrustation. Once the surface is completely dry, it can be sanded, carved with carving tools, or scored with nails or a knife.

6 Paint the encrustation with liquid acrylics, or polish it with shoe polish (see photo, right). When the paint or polish is dry, give the cover a final coat of paste wax. Carefully peel off any masking tape. Buff the book with rags when the paste wax is completely dry.

You can achieve a variety of effects using this method (see photos, below).

Above: Gwen Diehn, *Senso Unico*, 2001.

Above: The encrusted cover of Coral Jensen's journal adds inviting warmth and dimension to the book.

COLLAGE

Either hard or soft covers can be changed by collage. You can glue decorative papers, pressed leaves, fabric, or memorabilia to the cover of any book or journal.

You Will Need
– PVA
– Glue brush
– Newspapers
– Collage materials: paper, cloth, thin leather, memorabilia, etc.
– Soft, flat 1 inch (2.5 cm) paintbrush
– Polymer varnish, satin, flat, or gloss finish

Instructions

1 Cover the work surface with newspaper or scrap paper. Brush PVA all over the backs of the items to be collaged. Press collage items into place on the hard or softcover of your journal (see photo, below).

2 After the collage is dry, you can add any drawing or writing that you wish. Repeat for the other cover. When the entire book is dry, varnish with two coats of polymer varnish.

Marbled and handmade papers were collaged onto this cover.

LETTERING

Add a title to any book cover by carefully lettering on the surface with compatible ink or paint. If the surface is very shiny or rough, follow the directions below for making a label. You can put a title on the spine as well as on the cover of the book.

You Will Need
- Paper label
- Matte knife
- Ruler
- PVA
- Glue brush
- Polymer varnish
- Acrylic absorbent white ground*

•available where acrylic paints are sold

Instructions

1 Measure your paper label, and trace its shape on the cover of the book. Use a ruler and matte knife to carefully make a shallow cut around the traced outline. Your cut should be just deep enough to penetrate the outer layers of the cover material. Peel the outer layers of the cover material from inside the cut lines.

2 Using PVA, glue the label into place in the space you created in step 1.

3 Stencil or write in the title. Varnish the paper label with matte finish polymer varnish.

Variation

You can also write a title directly on the cover using contrasting or metallic finish media, such as metallic paints or pens.

Polly Smith, *Simon*, 2000-2001. Color photocopies, mementos, photographs, watercolor, and collage. Cover is a color scan of a hospital receiving blanket. PHOTO BY ARTIST

DRAWING

If your book has a smooth or slightly rough cardboard cover, draw and paint on it with waterproof pens or acrylics. To prepare a surface for paints, first paint on three layers of acrylic gesso. Let each layer dry completely, and sand in between layers.

To prepare a slick or shiny surface for pens or rubber stamps, paint a couple of layers of absorbent white ground onto the cover as a base layer. Let this base layer dry completely between coats and before drawing or stamping.

Coral Jensen, *Journal Cover*, 2001.

Emblem Books

Those of us who enjoy drawing in our journals (and writing in our sketchbooks) are part of a very long tradition. From early in the history of Western art, people have been trying to combine writing and pictures on the same sheet of parchment or paper, and the two systems of meaning-filled marks have existed in uneasy relationship to one another. Either the meaning of the page is conveyed mainly by the text, with the illustrations providing some enjoyable but nonessential embellishment, or the illustration is the most important element, with the text merely labeling or identifying it. Rarely have text and visuals formed a seamless and balanced whole. In fact, some contemporary linguists tell us that the mental processes needed to decode text are different from those that we use to make sense of images, which perhaps accounts for the sense of shifting gears that we often experience as we move between reading text and looking at images.

An early example of an attempt to combine text and image in an equal relationship is the 16th- and 17th-century emblem book. Emblems were combinations of a picture (either a woodcut or an engraving) and a motto, which served as a title and a short verse or prose passage. By reading the verse and viewing the image, the reader was able to interpret a moral meaning or lesson. Emblem books, which were collections of emblems, were a popular means of education throughout Europe at that time.

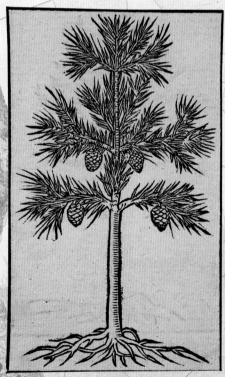 

From left: "Le Pin" and "L'Orengier" from *Alciato/Aneau Les Emblems*, 1549.

"The pine has no shoots from its roots; it is the sign of a man who dies without children."

"Oranges are of Venus, a sign of love, for the fruit of love is bittersweet."

Emblems of Love.
EMB. 25.

Emblemi d'Amore.

Emblemata Amatoria.
EMB. 25.

Invidia amoris comes.

Dum Canis os rodit socium quem diligit odit.

Envy accompanyes Love

Two you may see, like brothers sport and play,
As if their soules did in one poynt unite,
Throw but the bone cald woeman in the way,
How fiercely will thy grin, and snarl, & bite.

Invidia compagna d'Amore.

L'Amante vuol godersi la sua Diua,
Solo e non vuel soffrir alcun riuale,
Come il cane per un osso schiua,
Odia il compagno e lui vuol male.

Le Monarque et l'amoureux,
Ne ueulent point être deux.

L'Empire ny l'amour ne souffrent point d'égal,
Deux Héros pretendant à la même Couronne,
Deux Amans pleins de feu pour la même personne,
N'ont iamais regardé de bon oeil un riual.

Emblemes d'Amour.
G

What sets the emblem book apart from other illustrated books is the density of symbolism in the images. Some scholars consider them to be in part an attempt to create and define a pictographic language, something like ancient Egyptian hieroglyphics. In the world of medieval Europe, every plant, animal, insect, celestial body, and human figure was endowed with meaning that was beyond the literal meaning of the object. The secondary meanings were usually derived from the teachings and beliefs of the Christian church. A lily, for example, was not simply a sweet-smelling white flower, but was universally recognized as the embodiment of the attribute of purity. If a person appeared in a scene with a lily in her arms, the viewer understood the intention of the scene. The crescent moon in the sky, a scallop shell underfoot, or a lion and a lamb reclining on a distant rock promontory, all held symbolic meaning beyond the literal.

The reader of the emblem book read all of the symbols embedded in the picture as well as the literal meaning of the picture. So rich and many-layered were these images that the textual elements on the pages simply added another dimension, rather than provided a definition or explanation of the images. Many people couldn't read the text and depended completely on their knowledge of iconography or the meaning of the symbols to "read" the images. For them, the text was actually more decorative than meaning-filled.

The combination of deeply symbolic images and text in emblem books was inspired indirectly by Egyptian hieroglyphics. Since hieroglyphics were not decoded until the 19th century, they remained mysterious and indecipherable images to people during the Medieval and

Renaissance periods. In 1419, a monk discovered a manuscript from the fifth century. This manuscript was known as the "Hieroglyphica" of Horus Apollo and was found on the Greek island of Andros. When it was first discovered, it was believed to be a Greek translation of an Egyptian work that explained the secret meanings of Egyptian hieroglyphics. Although the manuscript later proved to be false, at the time of its discovery it was enormously influential and was one of the factors that led to the Renaissance idea that densely symbolic images could carry complex and subtle meanings.

Emblem books were printed throughout Europe in at least a dozen different languages from 1531 until around 1700. Many of them exist today in museums and rare book collections. They provide us with an unparalleled view of the daily life, ideas, morals, and art of the 16th and 17th centuries in Europe.

Illustration XXVIII, "No inward Griefe, Nor Outward Smart Can Overcome a Patient Heart," from George Wither's, *A Collection of Emblemes, Ancient and Moderne, Quickened with Metricall Illustrations, Both Morall and Divine: And Disposed into Lotteries, that Instruction, and Good Counsell, May Bee Furthered By an Honest and Pleasant Recreation*, 1635.

DVRIN. VICTRIA. PATIENTIA.

ILLVSTR. XXVIII.   Book. I.

Ome *Trees*, when Men oppresse their Aged Heads,
(With waighty Stones) they fructifie the more;
And, when upon some *Herbs*, the *Gard'ner* treads,
They thrive and prosper, better then before:
So, when the Kings of *Ægypt* did oppresse
The Sonnes of *Iacob*, through their Tyrannies;
Their Numbers, every day, did more encrease,
Till they grew greater then their Enemies.
So, when the *Iewes* and *Gentiles*, joyn'd their Powre
The *Lord*, and his *Annoynted*, to withstand;
(With raging *Furie*, lab'ring to devoure
And roote the *Gospel*, out of ev'ry Land)
The more they rag'd, conspired, and envy'd,
The more they slander'd, scorn'd, and murthered;
The more, the *Faithfull*, still, were multiply'd:
And, still, the further, their *Profession* spred.
Yea, so it spred, that quite it overthrew
Ev'n *Tyranny* it selfe; that, at the last,
The *Patience of the Saints*, most pow'rfull grew,
And *Persecutions* force, to ground was cast.
   The selfe-same Pow'r, true *Patience*, yet retaines,
And (though a thousand *Sufrings* wound the same)
She still hath *Hope* enough to ease her paynes;
That *Hope*, which keepeth off, all *Feare* and *Shame*:
For, 'tis not *Hunger*, *Cold*, nor *Fire*, nor *Steele*,
Nor all the *Scornes* or *Slanders*, we can heare,
Nor any *Torment*, which our *Flesh* can feele,
That conquers us; but, our owne Trayt'rous *Feare*.
   Where, *Honest Mindes*, and *Patient* Hearts, are Mates;
They grow victorious, in their *Hardest Fates*.

By

Preparing Pages

Preparing the pages of a blank book takes you further into a relationship with the pages themselves, so that before you even begin to write or make visual images in the book, you have set up an environment that is compatible with the kinds of ideas and emotions you intend for the book to communicate. Preparing a book's pages in advance also has the advantage of doing away with their glaring blankness, so that the page you face each day already has some mark on it to which you can respond. Starting pages in advance saves time. If the pages have already been prepared, you don't need to spend any time laying a base for the page when you sit down to make a journal entry or work in your scrapbook. In addition, an underlayer or substratum can make the page richer and more complex.

You can prepare a few pages at a time or just prepare every other page. It's always a good idea to leave some blank pages for projects that need a plain background. Use a light touch to prepare your pages. Lighter colors and subtle textures will not interfere with what you later write or draw on the page. Dark or bright colors and aggressive textures can create visual noise when another layer is put on top of them. If you want a very strong underlayer for a particular purpose, be prepared to use strong materials, such as heavy black pen, large lettering, bold stamps, opaque gouache, or collage on top of these stronger background layers.

The page-preparation techniques in this section are divided into two categories: wet processes and dry processes. Certain processes work better with some kinds of papers than others, so experiment until you find a texture and look that inspires you.

Andrea A. Peterson, *Penland Sketchbook*, 1993. Hemp, butterfly wing, pastels, and ink. PHOTO BY ARTIST

WET PROCESSES

Wet processes work best on medium to heavyweight paper. If you're in doubt, experiment on a page in the middle of the book, and cut the page out if it doesn't work (see page 35 for directions for removing a page from a book). All wet processes cause most papers to warp and cockle to some degree, and some may not flatten completely, even when pressed flat after they're dry. If it's important to you to have completely flat pages and the paper you're using doesn't dry flat, skip this section and use the dry processes described in the next section to prepare your pages.

You can prepare several pages one after another, but be sure to keep sheets of newspaper or blotters between all wet sheets while you're working. When you finish, stand the book up to dry with the pages fanned out. Some pages may dry wrinkled and cockled, but once they're dry you can press them by closing the book and placing it under a pile of heavy books or bricks. The pages will flatten out more or less, depending on the kind of paper and on the way in which the book is bound. As an alternative, you can speed the drying process by using a hair dryer to blow-dry individual pages.

Colleen Stanton, *Untitled Journal Page*, 2000. PHOTO BY ELYSE WEINGARTEN

POURED ACRYLIC

Acrylic paints have the useful quality of drying permanently. Once they're dry, you can add watercolor on top of them with no danger of muddying the acrylic layer. Liquid acrylics are especially good for pouring spontaneous, random layers.

You Will Need
- Liquid acrylics in several colors
- Empty detergent or other kinds of plastic squirt bottles, one for each color
- Medicine dropper and a small jar (optional)
- Blotters, 2 inches (5.1 cm) longer and wider than book pages
- Newspapers (NOT the shiny inserts), equal to the size of the page (optional)

Instructions

1 Mix a few drops of liquid acrylic paint into a few ounces of water in a squirt bottle or small jar (if using a medicine dropper). Shake the bottle or stir the jar to completely mix the paint into the water. Squirt or drip out a little onto scrap paper, and blot it to test the color. If it's too dark, add more water; if it's too light, add more paint. Add other colors of paint to adjust the color mix, if necessary.

2 When the color looks right, place a blotter, or several sheets of newspaper, under the page you want to prepare. Squirt a small amount of watery paint onto the paper. If you want, use two or more colors at a time, squirting a little of each color in different spots on the page. The watery paint will form a small puddle, unless the paper is not sized, in which case the paint will quickly sink into the paper.

3 Quickly fold the facing page over, and press on it to squeeze and spread the puddle. The object is to spread the wet paint around, so you wind up with an inkblot pattern. If you don't want a symmetrical blot on the two facing pages, use a blotter instead of the facing page to press the puddle.

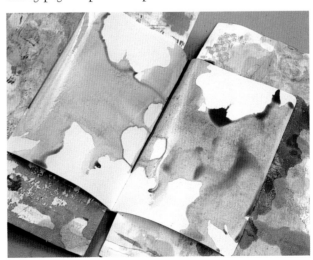

4 You can add more paint, blotting and pressing each time. If the paper is on the thin side, it will probably look wet and fragile when wet. Even heavier paper will wrinkle to some degree while it's wet. Handle the book carefully during this stage of the process. Keep sheets of newspaper or blotter between all wet sheets while you're working. Follow the instructions on page 54 for drying pages flat.

Variations

Add metallics or different paint colors for a rich look. Different paints look different on different page textures, so experiment to achieve the look you want.

WATERCOLOR WASH

A watercolor wash, unlike an acrylic wash, can be rewet after it has dried. This means that if you're painting on top of watercolor, there will be some mixing of colors. You can exploit this quality to good effect, or you can work faster and with a light touch to minimize color mixing.

You Will Need
– Watercolors
– Water
– Mixing jar
– Watercolor brush
– Mixing tray (any smooth, flat, non-porous surface will do: an old dinner plate, an old pie tin, etc.)
– Blotter or stack of newspapers

Instructions

1 Mix up a watery batch of watercolor paint and water on the mixing tray.

2 Put a blotter or some sheets of newspaper beneath the page you're going to prepare. Paint the color smoothly onto the page. You can add a border, as in the photo below, do a plain wash (add another color or layer after the first dries for more depth), paint an overall pattern, or extend your pattern over two pages.

3 Prepare pages one after the other, following the instructions for drying on page 54.

Variation

For a subtle texture, dab paint on one page in a random pattern, then touch it with the opposite page, spreading the paint (see photo, right).

WATERCOLOR WASH WITH PLASTIC WRAP

There are several effects that you can get from manipulating wet watercolor washes. The next two processes will change ordinary watercolor washes into mysterious surfaces with elegant, spontaneous passages.

You Will Need

– Blotters or newspapers
– Watercolors
– Watercolor brush
– Mixing tray
– Sponge
– Plastic wrap

Instructions

1 Place a blotter or some sheets of newspaper beneath the page you're going to prepare.

2 Mix up a batch of watercolor and water in a mixing tray.

3 Sponge clean water over the entire page to dampen it.

4 Working quickly, paint the page with the wash. You can also pour on a couple of different colored puddles and let them flow together.

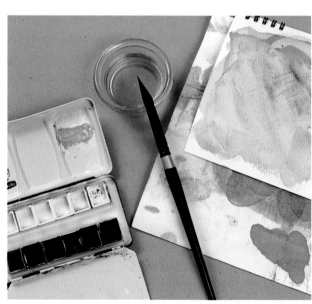

5 Before the paint dries, lay a sheet of plastic wrap over the entire painted surface, scrunching the plastic wrap into wrinkles. Leave the plastic wrap in place for about 5 minutes.

Variation

You can achieve interesting effects by adding table salt to a wet watercolor wash.

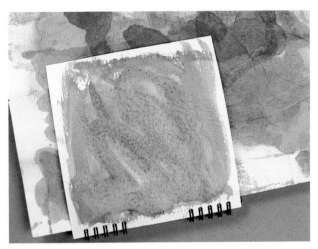

6 Peel off the plastic wrap. The resulting design is caused by paint darkening in the places where it was in contact with the plastic wrap. Follow the directions on page 54 for drying and pressing the book.

Working quickly before the paint dries, sprinkle table salt in a random arrangement over the painting. Wherever the salt lands, it will absorb water in such a way that the area around the salt crystal will be lighter than the surrounding area.

DRY PROCESSES

These are actually *relatively* dry processes. They work well for thin paper that can't withstand the large amount of water used in the wet processes, and equally well for heavier papers. None of these processes warp or cockle paper.

Because these are only relatively dry processes, you should treat them as you do wet processes until your book is dry. Follow the instructions on page 54 for drying pages.

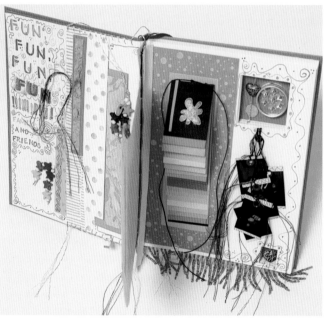

Sheila Cunningham, *The Orange Journal,* 2001. Metallic thread, grommets, photos, hand-carved stamps, and metallic pens. PHOTO BY ARTIST

SPONGE-PAINTED ACRYLICS, GOUACHE, OR WATERCOLORS

Sponge painting transfers a small amount of paint to the page and spreads it into a thin, delicate layer, leaving no brush strokes. You can also leave sponge prints or sponge through a stencil to make a regular pattern.

You Will Need
- Liquid acrylics, watercolors, or gouache (opaque watercolors)
- Water
- Mixing jar
- Mixing tray
- Flat sponge, such as a plastic dishwashing sponge
- Masking tape (optional)
- Scrap paper
- Stencil, large-holed needlepoint canvas, wire screen, lacey or openwork cloth or paper (optional)
- Hair dryer (optional)

Instructions

1 Mix the colors that you want to use on the mixing tray. If you're using liquid acrylics, don't dilute them. If you're using watercolors or gouache, dilute them just enough to form paint that is about the same

consistency as heavy cream. If you want a clean border, first put strips of masking tape over areas of the page that you don't want to have paint on them (see photo, bottom right, opposite page). To prevent the masking tape from tearing the surface of the paper, first stick it to your pants leg or some other piece of cloth to remove some of the tack.

2 Tap the sponge into the paint to pick up a small amount. Then tap or daub the sponge onto a piece of scrap paper until it makes the kind of marks you want. You can adjust the way the paint looks by how much pressure you place on the sponge, as well as by the amount of paint you pick up.

3 Tap and daub the sponge all over the page that you're preparing, picking up more paint and different colors as necessary. Dry the pages in the manner described on page 54.

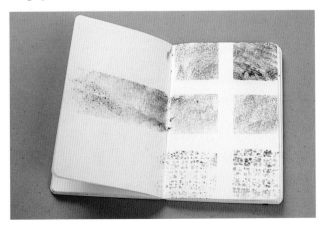

Variation

To sponge through a stencil, lay the piece of cloth, screen, or paper over the page to be prepared. Follow steps 1 through 3, then peel off the stencil and dry the page as usual.

ACRYLIC MESH PRINT

This process results in a soft, grid-like pattern that can be an interesting underlayer for writing and drawing.

You Will Need
– Plastic needlepoint canvas, #7 or larger-holed
– Liquid acrylic paints
– Small sponge

Instructions

1 Use the sponge to rub a light coat of acrylic all over one side of the plastic canvas.

2 Carefully lay the canvas, painted side down, on top of the page to be prepared. Being careful not to shift the canvas, press firmly all over the back of the canvas to offset the paint onto the paper.

3 Peel the canvas off the paper, and dry as usual.

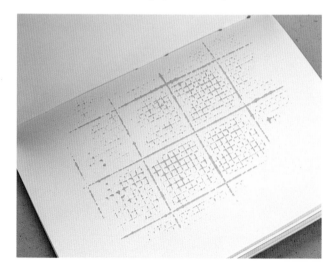

Variations

You can achieve different effects by using mesh with larger or smaller patterns. The texture of your paper will also affect the outcome of the process.

SPONGED-ON STAMP PAD INK

Pigment-type stamp pad ink can be sponged on so that graduated tones result. Cotton cosmetic removal pads or fine-grained soft sponges leave no stroke marks and give smooth coverage.

You Will Need
– Masking tape
– Cotton cosmetic removal pads or smooth sponge
– Pigment-dyed stamp pad or pads
– Scrap paper
– Wax paper (optional)

Instructions

1 First, mask off a border or sections of the page that will not have color, unless you want the entire page to be filled with color. To remove some of the tack from the tape, first stick it to your pants leg or another piece of cloth.

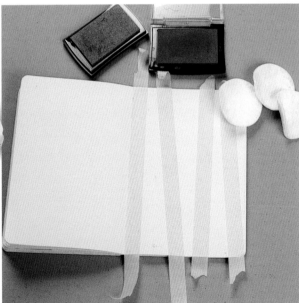

2 Daub a cotton pad onto the stamp pad, then tap it a few times on a piece of scrap paper to remove any dark blotches of ink. Then begin gently tapping and wiping the ink onto the page. You can rub in circles with considerable pressure to get smooth coverage. Increasing pressure results in darker tones.

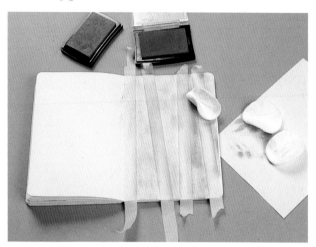

3 When the page is sufficiently covered, peel off any tape. Place a clean sheet of wax paper or scrap paper between the sheets of paper prepared in this way until the ink is completely dry. Drying may take from a few hours to a few days, depending on the kind of paper you use.

Variation

Try taping the page in different patterns (diagonal, grid, column) or mixing colors for a clouded effect (see photo, below).

COPIER TRANSFERS

An easy way to get an image onto a page is to make a color or black and white photocopy of it and then transfer the image into your journal. Once the copy is transferred, you can draw or paint right on top of it, adding color, simplifying forms, and otherwise altering the image to suit your purposes.

You Will Need

- A fresh photocopy
- Citrus-based gel-style paint stripper*
- Paintbrush
- Wooden spoon for burnishing
- Drafting tape (optional)

*This product is safe to use indoors without a lot of ventilation, but read all product cautions before using.

Instructions

1 Begin by laying the copy face down on the journal page. You might tape it lightly to the page with drafting tape to keep it from moving. Generously brush the back of the copy with citrus-based, gel-style paint stripper.

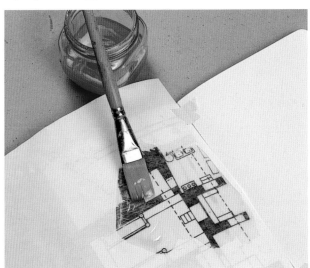

2 Rub or burnish the back of the copy with the rounded bowl of a wooden or metal spoon. Be very careful not to shift the copy at all. You can check the progress of the transfer by holding the copy in place and carefully lifting one corner at a time to see how well the image is transferring.

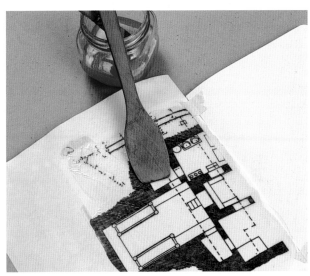

3 If the transfer isn't dark enough, either burnish some more, or add more gel. Fresh, new copies work better than old copies. A successful copy transfer will be dark enough to show some details .

STAMP PATTERN

Small rubber stamps can be used to make individual marks, almost like brush strokes, in an overall pattern.

You Will Need
- Commercial or homemade rubber stamp in a simple design
- Dye-type ink stamp pad*
- Scrap paper or wax paper (optional)

*Note: Dye-based inks dry faster than pigment inks; it's okay to use pigment inks for this, but be aware that they will take longer to dry.

Instructions
Ink the stamp, and stamp it all over the page in a regular or irregular pattern. If you are using pigment ink, interleaf the page with wax paper or clean scrap paper until it is dry.

Variations
Give your page more dimension with a stamp border that extends well into the page.

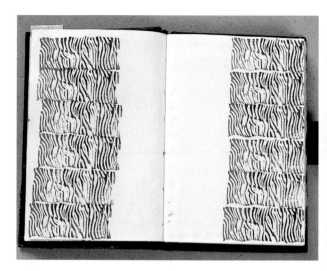

You can also stamp page stubs to turn them into design elements.

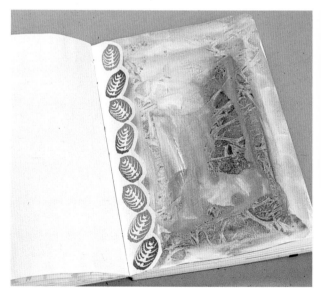

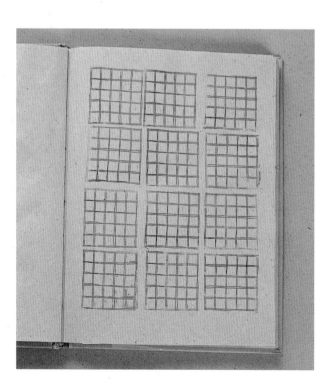

DRAWING CLOSER:
NATURE JOURNALING

"What I have not drawn, I have never really seen," writes Frederick Franck in his book *The Zen of Seeing* (1973, Random House). Franck's statement is in many ways the basis of the practice of nature journaling. From ancient people who drew carefully observed animals on the walls of caves, to 19th-century amateur naturalists who avidly drew their collections of insects and plants, drawing has long been a primary way to learn about and record the natural world.

Interestingly, photography has never really replaced drawing as a way of knowing or as a way of accurately representing nature. Certainly nature has been extensively photographed, and the resulting images have been used in many ways. But photography is too fast to replace the process of drawing; the same kind of slow, intimate, developmental seeing does not take place. It's still true that if you want to learn about the buds on your night-blooming cereus plant, drawing is one of the best ways to do so. A drawing records them with greater clarity because it lets you omit background clutter while emphasizing details such as the little spurs that barely show against the side of the bud stem. Drawings are still often used for identification manuals because of their clarity and ability to isolate certain elements while eliminating the extraneous.

Keeping a nature journal will enhance your enjoyment of nature, and you don't have to be an artist to keep one. Hannah Hinchman, a long-time nature journaler and the author of *A Trail Through Leaves: The Journal as a Path to Place* (1997, W. W. Norton & Co.), believes that drawing should be taught to every child alongside reading and writing and given equal emphasis. In Betty Edwards's groundbreaking book *Drawing on the Right Side of the Brain* (1999, JP Tarcher), Edwards says that in our culture we act as though visual skills were rare and mysterious and only available to a few highly gifted "artists." In reality, Edwards, Hinchman, and others maintain, everyone can and should learn to draw; and everyone would do so if they were given good materials (instead of markers, blunt crayons, and cheap paper), and were asked simple questions that would help them see and draw what they see.

I know from my own experience of teaching drawing for many years that everyone can learn to draw. The tools that most help me teach students to draw are, actually, a few questions. It helps to have a teacher, but you can simply ask them of yourself as

Hannah Hinchman, *Wind River, Number 13*, June 1989. Printed with permission of the artist

you set out to draw that night-blooming cereus bud before it does its one-night-stand-blooming performance and disappears forever. Here are the questions:

1. What, actually, do I see? (What is its general shape? What does this shape remind me of? How much of it do I want to draw?)
2. How wide is it compared to its height?
3. How big is this part compared to that part?
4. Is this part a true vertical or horizontal, and if not, how far off the vertical or horizontal is it?
5. If I dropped a plumb line (a string with a weight tied to the end) from this point, what would it hit lower down? If I ran a straight horizontal across from this point, where would it intersect this part?

To answer these questions, which you will ask over and over again, whenever something looks wrong or even slightly off, and especially when you start a new drawing, you'll need a pencil or other straight stick at least 6 inches (15.2 cm) long. To make comparative measures, you will hold the stick in one hand with your elbow straight. (This is important, as you need to keep the relative distance between the object, your eye, and the stick the same throughout measuring.) Close one eye. Place the tip of the stick so that it appears to touch one edge of the object, then place your thumbnail at the apparent other edge of the object. Holding this unit of measurement—and keeping your elbow straight—see how many of these units fit across the expanse you're measuring. For example, I might determine the size of the width of a stem, and then see how many stem-widths (the unit) long the bud is.

To determine how far off a vertical or horizontal something is, hold the stick horizontally beneath or vertically alongside the object, close one eye, and estimate how far off the vertical or horizontal the object (or the part of the object) is.

To use a plumb line or horizontal straight lines, use the stick in either a vertical or horizontal orientation.

With practice you'll get better and better at estimating measures and will soon no longer need to actually measure so often. But even after years of practice you'll from time to time look at a drawing in progress and say, "It looks funny. Something's off." That's when you need to measure, and you'll easily discover what you need to do to fix things.

Of course there is more that you can learn about drawing, but these few tools will get you started. The key to learning is practice. If you find that you really like to draw and you want to learn more refinements, I highly recommend Hannah Hinchman's and Betty Edwards's books.

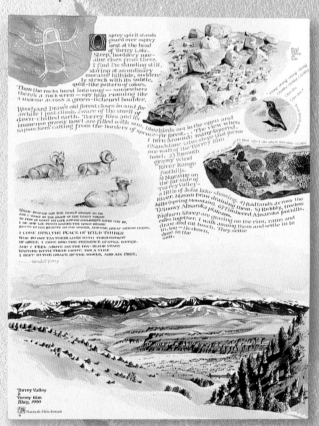

Hannah Hinchman, *Torrey Valley and Torrey Rim*, May 1990. Printed with permission of the artist

LAYOUTS

Now that you've gathered materials, customized your blank book, and prepared the pages, you can begin to focus on filling the pages with your thoughts and reflections, drawings, photographs, mementos, scraps, and whatever else you wish. But where do you start, and how do you arrange everything? Planning the layout of your page in advance will help you to make the most of the space you have available, and help you to achieve an effective and appealing visual presentation. You may even find that it helps you to organize your thoughts and express yourself in ways you hadn't even considered.

In this section of the book, we'll review different layout alternatives and discuss the characteristics of each. You'll learn how using one layout over another can help give a page a different feel—make it seem bigger, provide a sense of order, or complement the emotional nature of a written entry. You'll see examples of each kind of layout so you can review how different journalers have applied a variety of layouts to their own material.

The layout of a page is the foundation of its design. More specifically, layout refers to the proportioning and balancing of elements (text, illustrations, headlines, or titles, etc.), that give a page a certain unity and help it to achieve its purpose. Graphic designers work very intentionally with layout; journalers rarely consider it. Most often, layout is done intuitively, or the journaler or scrapbook maker falls into a habit of repeating the same layout on many pages in a book. But attention to layout can help you express an idea or emotion just as it helps graphic designers sell products or tell stories. Even though a prepared page is not as intimidating as a completely blank one, you still have to decide how to take the next step. Awareness of layout possibilities can make the first steps of page building easier. Sometimes you can unstick a debilitating creative block simply by experimenting with a different layout.

The materials used in a book must have certain characteristics in order to yield good and lasting results. When it comes to page layout, the only limitation is your imagination. Let the following ideas get you started; then combine and customize these ideas as you go along. Before you know it, you will be returning each day to a rich, many-layered book that will continue to grow and inspire you each time you open it.

Kelcey Loomer, *Untitled Journal Page*, 2000. Collage, pen and ink.
PHOTO BY ELYSE WEINGARTEN

Full-Page Designs

Using a solid block of text or a drawing or painting that fills a page is a popular strategy used by journalers and sketchbook artists. But also consider some variations within the full-page design, such as creating borders.

Andrea Peterson, *Albania Sketchbook*, 1992. Tempera, chalk, and pencil. PHOTO BY ARTIST

BLEEDS

A design that comes to the edges of a page is called a *bleed*. A bleed can make text, as well as visual material, seem to be part of a bigger whole, a bigger scene. It can give a sense of openness to the content and make it seem to grow beyond the page.

Christine Toriello, *Untitled Journal Page*, 2000. Collage, pen and ink. PHOTO BY ELYSE WEINGARTEN

Collen Stanton, *Untitled Journal Page*, 2000. Pen over watercolor. PHOTO BY ELYSE WEINGARTEN

BORDERS

An edge, either plain or decorated, frames a page of text or illustration and in some ways confines the material on the page. It can make each page seem like a separate entity. A decorated border is especially good at highlighting or emphasizing the material within it. A plain border can invite editorial comments and later additions.

Blair Gulledge, *Untitled Journal Page*, 2000. Watercolor and pen.
PHOTO BY ELYSE WEINGARTEN

Kelcey Loomer, *Untitled Journal Page,* 2000. Collage, pen, watercolor.
PHOTO BY ELYSE WEINGARTEN

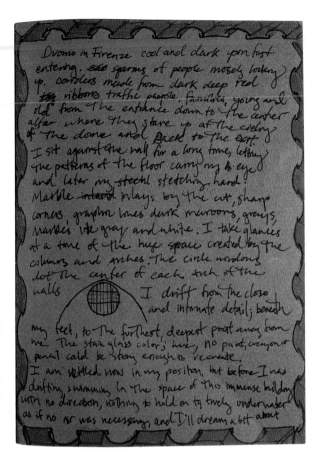

Laura Carter, *Untitled Journal Page*, 2000. Pen, colored pencil on blue paper. PHOTO BY ELYSE WEINGARTEN

Kelcey Loomer, *Untitled Journal Page*, 2000. Watercolor, pen.
PHOTO BY ELYSE WEINGARTEN

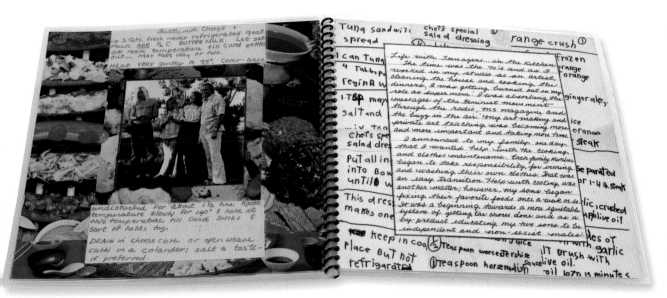

Mary Ellen Long, *In the Kitchen*, 2000. Collage and pen. PHOTO BY ARTIST

Escaping from Flatland

Edward Tufte has spent much of his life studying and teaching the art and science of information design, the visual presentation of information. He has written, designed, and published several award-winning books on the subject, two of which are of particular interest to visual-verbal journal keepers: *Visual Explanations* (1997, Graphics Press) and *Envisioning Information* (1990, Graphics Press).

According to Tufte, the main challenge of information design is to represent the multidimensional visual world of experience and measurement on the two-dimensional, flat surface of a piece of paper, which he calls "Flatland." His books are elegant examples of how to do just that, and in them he includes many analyses of various attempts to present information in visual form. After years of analyzing visuals that clarify and those that obscure, he has developed several strategies for information design that can help us escape from Flatland. Three of these seem particularly appropriate for journalers.

One of Tufte's basic principles of good information design is based on an old maxim known as Occam's Razor: "What can be done with fewer is done in vain with more." Tufte's application of Occam's Razor is what he calls *the strategy of the smallest effective difference*: Make all visual distinctions as subtle as possible, but still clear and effective. This strategy is easy to understand in the case of grids. Let's imagine that you want to use a grid to present some information you've gathered about several different kinds of birds that you've seen at your bird feeder over several months. You could draw a heavy, dark grid and place the information in the boxes

Edward Tufte, *Colored T-Shirts*, from his book *Envisioning Information* (Graphics Press, 1990).

using bright red pen. The result would be filled with what Tufte calls visual static. The jarring grid lines would compete loudly with the information contained within them, resulting in an unpleasant, overly bright display.

The strategy of smallest effective difference suggests that when you prepare pages, you use the lightest and subtlest tones (unless in a particular case you know that you want the page to be brighter and more forceful than usual). Light underlayers are easier to distinguish from whatever is placed on top of them, leaving the possibility of more range in the kinds of marks that you make on each prepared page.

Following the strategy of smallest effective difference, you would draw the grid with pale lines, just dark enough to be distinguished from the paper tone. Information could be added to this subtle grid in fine, crisp, black print that would be easily distinguished from the grid lines. The result would be easier to read and more elegant and pleasing to look at. In the example shown here (see photo, opposite page), the white space between the elements functions perfectly as an implied grid.

A second Tufte strategy is to use what he calls *small multiples*. In a design using small multiples, the same design structure is repeated for all the images. Small multiples can be arranged side by side and one on top of the other on the same page, allowing the viewer to see all at once and make comparisons more easily than if the designs were on separate pages. In Tufte's *T-Shirts* (see photo, opposite page), the t-shirts and vests are all identical in size and shape. The constancy in design allows the viewer to focus easily on the changing element, in this case the color combinations.

You might use the strategy of small multiples if you are comparing the colors of olives in a marketplace or if you are showing the variation in butterflies that have visited your garden this week. Tufte says that the strategy of small multiples gets to the heart of visual reasoning in that it helps us see, distinguish, and choose.

A third strategy that Tufte discusses is what he calls *visual confections*. A visual confection is an arrangement, a gathering of many different visual events. Whereas an illustration is similar in content to a snapshot (it shows what is happening at a particular time in a single narrative or story), a confection brings together elements from several different story lines, narratives, or times and puts them in one place at the same time, even though these elements (or people or events) have not been and couldn't logically be together in one place at the same time. A confection differs from a chart, diagram, or map in that it does not place the people, events, or objects into conventional formats.

There are two strategies for assembling confections: One is the imaginary scene, often filled with symbolic objects or people. The other is compartments, in which boxes or bubbles or sometimes just space separate the elements. Many confections use both strategies simultaneously, with compartments holding elements in a scene that unifies the various compartments.

Tufte's books are filled with wonderful reflections on the visual representation of information. You can find out more about them from Graphics Press, PO Box 430, Cheshire, CT 06410.

Grids

Grids are basic organizing systems that consist of the repetition of a certain unit. They project a sense of order and control. When used with strongly emotional material, they can introduce an edgy contrast that heightens the impact of the design. You can create grids in an infinite variety of sizes and shapes, depending on what you want to express.

Gwen Diehn, *Untitled Journal Page*, 2000. Watercolor, cork stamps, pen. PHOTO BY ELYSE WEINGARTEN

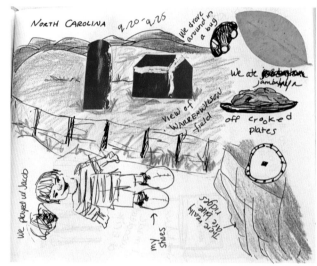

Kerstin Vogdes, *Untitled Journal* Page, 2001. Watercolor, pen

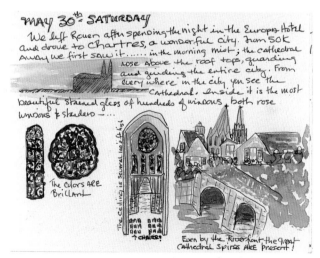

Dorothy Herbert, *Untitled Journal Page*, 2000. Watercolor, pen.
PHOTO BY ELYSE WEINGARTEN

Susan Saling, *Untitled Journal Page*, 2000. Collage, watercolor, pen

Mandalas

A mandala is a symmetrical design based on a circle, with a central focal point; it can cover one page or be a two-page spread. A mandala is a good way to highlight a main point as well as show supporting ideas, images, or context. It's also a very calm layout and lends itself well to content with a meditative focus.

Gwen Diehn, *Untitled Journal Page*, 2000. Watercolor, stamps made from foam rubber earplugs and corks. PHOTO BY ELYSE WEINGARTEN

Laurie Adams, *Untitled Journal Page*, 2000. Colored pencil, pastel, pen and ink

Colleen Stanton, *Untitled Journal Page*, 2000. Watercolor, pen. PHOTO BY ELYSE WEINGARTEN

Columns

Columns can be of any width. They can be made of text, image, or a combination of the two. Columns and grids can be combined on the same page. Like grids, columns connote a certain orderliness. They also make long text passages easier to read because they shorten the length of each line. Columns are a good layout to use when many small visuals illustrate the same block of text or when you want to make comparisons among many ideas or units.

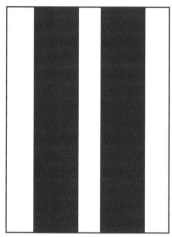

Collen Stanton, *Untitled Journal Page*, 2000. Watercolor, pen.
PHOTO BY ELYSE WEINGARTEN

Colleen Stanton, *Untitled Journal Page*, 2000. Watercolor pencil, pen.
PHOTO BY ELYSE WEINGARTEN

Coranna Beene, *Untitled Journal Page,* 2000. Collage of cut train tickets written over with pen, on colored vellum pages. PHOTO BY ELYSE WEINGARTEN

Gwen Diehn, *Untitled Journal Page,* 2000. Watercolor pencil, pen. PHOTO BY ELYSE WEINGARTEN

Diagonals

Diagonals are always more emotional and attract more attention than the horizontals and verticals of grids and columns. Their inherent motion and instability communicate action and emotion. Diagonals need not be simple straight lines. Jagged and curved diagonals can be even more powerful and evocative.

Gwen Diehn, *Untitled Journal Page,* 2000. Watercolor, pen, gold foil and sugar wrapper. PHOTO BY ELYSE WEINGARTEN

Laura Carter, *Untitled Journal Page,* 2000. Soil mixed with PVA; pressed leaf, pens. PHOTO BY ELYSE WEINGARTEN

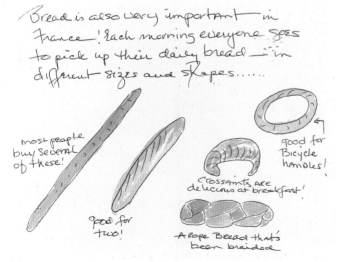

Dorothy Herbert, *Untitled Journal Page*, 2000. Watercolor, pen. PHOTO BY ELYSE WEINGARTEN

Organic Shapes

These are curved shapes that feel more natural than the abstract forms of columns, grids, and even diagonals. Organic shapes flow and melt, grow, evolve, and meander.

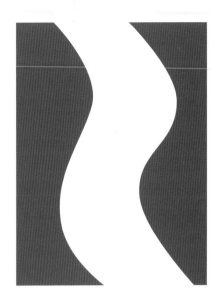

Dorothy Herbert, *Untitled Journal Page,* 2000. Watercolor, pen. PHOTO BY ELYSE WEINGARTEN

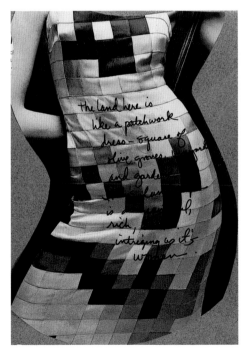

Christine Toriello, *Untitled Journal Page,* 2000. Collage, pen. PHOTO BY ELYSE WEINGARTEN

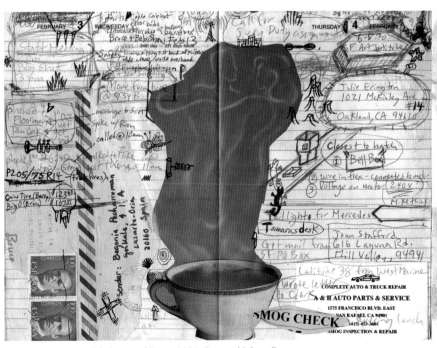

Bruce Kremer, *Untitled Journal Page,* 2001. Pen and ink, collage.

Cutouts and Add-Ons

Although not strictly considered layout elements, cutouts and add-ons introduce complexity and surprises. Cutouts can link pages and the ideas on them and thereby create the effect of a third and even fourth dimension in a book. They can highlight certain text and visuals. Consider cutting windows through from one page to the next, or cutting the corners and edges of pages, so the page corners and edges behind it can be seen. You might also glue or stitch on foldout pages or elements that extend from the page. You can attach small booklets or pockets to pages for a hypertext effect.

Laura Carter, *Untitled Journal Page,* 2000. Watercolor and cutout vellum page. PHOTO BY ELYSE WEINGARTEN

Coranna Beene, *Untitled Journal Pages,* 2000. Watercolor painted on white vellum over pen and watercolor; collage and pen on front of colored paper pocket. PHOTO BY ELYSE WEINGARTEN

Laurie Adams, *Costa Rica Journal Page,* 2000. Colored paper cut into leaf forms over colored pen, colored pencils

Nina Bagley, *Untitled Journal Page,* 2000. Collage, metallic pens, rubber stamps, metallic ink

WRITING SMALL

by Ann Turkle

Writing in a journal when you are considering page design may present some challenges, but it also introduces many opportunities. The decorated or visually defined page may invite words the way the stark white of an untouched page never would. If you aren't sure where to begin or what to write in your journal, start small. One of the most common complaints about journal-keeping of any kind is that it takes too much time. The verbal collecting you may do for a journal can fit so neatly into moments of available time that this objection will fall away, and, as it does, the value of the writing may become so apparent that making time for it is easier. Here are a few suggestions for approaching the written aspect of your journal.

WORK SMALL

There is no denying we have many small openings of time in our day. We wait at the stoplight, in the checkout line at the supermarket, for our e-mail connection to come online, or for a return phone call. These "in between" moments can leave us tapping our toes in impatience, but they can also allow us to turn with pen in hand to a small notebook or 3 x 5-inch (7.6 x 12.7 cm) card kept close at hand. It may seem a little tedious or obsessive to get into the habit of making observations or brief reflections throughout your day, but gradually this practice can yield great results: you'll learn to pay attention and be aware of what is going on around you, not just what is going on in your head.

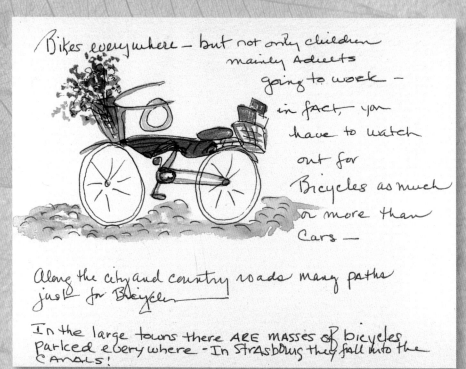

Dorothy Herbert, *Untitled Journal Page*, 2000. Watercolor, pen and ink. PHOTO BY ELYSE WEINGARTEN

and so the subway system in Rome displays the
similar social-governmental problems of homelessness that America
has. I didn't ever see
exit any men. All women and
children and pregnant
women, and a woman with no leg. How much
longer can I endure turning my head, thinking
another day-saying sorry no, watching
the annoyed or closed off faces of
the people around me
being begged to.
girl around my
age with a flat
belly leaning against
the cement wall
so resignedly
makes my heart
pound and my
eyes water. I want
to talk to them,
but I don't know
any words. gift for
I still walked past
them and came
home with 13,000 lire
in my
pocket and want a
gelato. I don't think I will ever be numb to
this. What can I do. One person?

Kelcey Loomer,
*Untitled Journal
Page*, 2000.
Watercolor, pen
and ink. PHOTO BY
ELYSE WEINGARTEN

Choose a convenient method for collecting your observations. Plain-paper notepads come as small as business cards, and range in size from 2 x 3½ inches (5.1 x 8.9 cm) to 6 x 4 inches (15.2 x 10.2 cm) to 7 x 5½ inches (17.8 x 14 cm), the same size as a daily planner. You can easily carry a few 3 x 5-inch (7.6 x 12.7 cm) cards or a tiny notebook with many pages. Since any of these options are small and easy to buy or make, you may want several so they are available in the places those openings of time happen—in the car, at the telephone or the computer, in your handbag or briefcase, or, best of all, in your pocket. Your collector notebook may go many places your larger journal would not easily fit, so you don't need to be quite so obvious about using it if you are at first a little shy about working on your journal in public. If someone asks what you are doing, you can always respond by saying "Oh, just making a list," because you may be doing precisely that.

STARTING A COLLECTION OF THOUGHTS

Writing exercises can bear a close resemblance to drawing exercises. The goal is to focus and to record the object of your attention. Although part of your aim may be to be more present or more aware in your surroundings, you don't want to ignore what you are thinking. In a sense, you may be opening a door to allow flashes of connection to come to you.

"Nonwriters" may perceive "writerly" creativity as something that happens in a writer's studio, or at least at the keyboard, but the beginnings of works (poems, verbal sketches, memoirs) are the quick apprehensions you will lose if you do not write them down: the perfect pattern of the cups and glasses stacked on the waiter's tray as he sets the café tables for dinner;

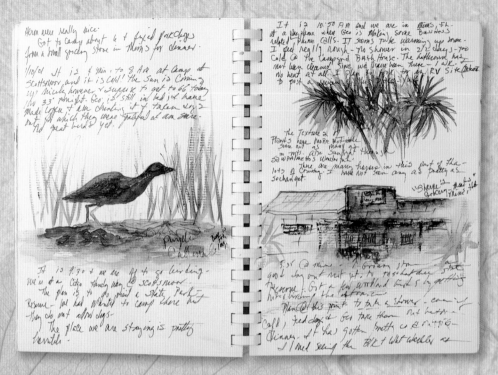

Elizabeth Ellison, *Untitled Journal Page*, 2000. Watercolor, pen and ink.

the almost conversational tone of the crows' exchange outside your window at daybreak; or the delighted smile of a six-year-old picking out a box of crayons as part of her back-to-school shopping. Tiny things may provide images and associations to build upon.

MAKE LISTS

Lists are liberating. They are much easier to generate than carefully constructed sentences, and they give us an opportunity to discover patterns, similarities, and differences. List every flower you have seen blooming today. Record the names of the tree species in your yard. Look over your lists and try to determine patterns which may evolve from similar sounds or a visual memory of color.

DESCRIBE

Try using very descriptive language to record your observations. For example: One morning I came upon a pretty box turtle about the size of a large coffee cup, as she sat between the broccoli and the tomato plants in my garden. She looked up at me with gold eyes, perfectly coordinated with the gold and greenish brown of her shell.

WITNESS

As you people-watch, try to record the actions of those you observe. Sitting on a park bench, I observed four children running through a puddle left by a recent rainstorm. First, they ran keeping their feet low to create a wake, then took huge steps, stomping up the biggest splash possible, and finally they ran and slid. They took turns initiating the action, almost the way members of a jazz ensemble take turns improvising.

LISTEN

Eavesdrop, record dialogue, and listen to what your surroundings tell you. I lived for two years on a corner in a residential neighborhood in Tallahassee, Florida. Gradually, I realized that I could describe that neighborhood, the time of day, the season, and the weather just by listening. The bus service to my corner started at about 7:00 a.m. and ended in the early evening, each pass punctuated by the distinctive squeal of brakes. The magnolia tree outside my bedroom window dropped its leaves with a sound almost as decisive as smashing plates. And as the direction of the wind changed, so did the approach that planes took toward the local airport, adding the rush of jet engines overhead. How would you describe the distinctive qualities of your neighborhood by sound? Can those sounds be made visible?

Once, sitting in a booth in a restaurant waiting for my meal to be served, I overheard a conversation between two couples, retirees. Without turning to look, I visualized them, making notes and a small sketch on a notecard, entirely on the strength of their voices and their way of speaking.

COLLECTING AND PLEASURE

An unintended payoff of paying attention is that we simply begin to take pleasure in our noticing, and suddenly, the collecting notebook becomes a "pleasure journal," the repository for unexpected moments of delight. Whereas you once fumed over the moments wasted on the price check for the patron in front of you in line, there is now the opportunity to quickly observe the precarious efforts of the five-year-old unloading the shopping cart, one item at a time, into the hands of the checker who is dutifully saying "thank you" at each handoff.

Colleen Stanton, *Untitled Journal Page*, 2000. Collage and pen.

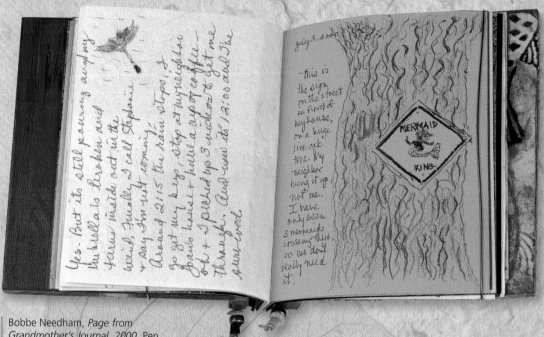

Bobbe Needham, *Page from Grandmother's Journal, 2000.* Pen and ink, colored pencil, crayon. Journal by Coral Jensen

FROM PATTERN TO METAPHOR

Collecting material in notebooks before transferring it into your journal allows you a lot of options. You may transfer material into the journal in many different ways, adding layers not only to the physical presentation, but to your appreciation and understanding of what you have collected. You may simply paste in a page of observations, or recopy it, then elaborate, reflect, or comment on the article you've added.

The interplay between the visual and the verbal elements of a journal often provides opportunities to explore metaphors. The kinship of images and words can suggest themes or motifs. Figures of speech that you remember from English class can come alive when words and images meet and influence each other. As you pay attention to your emerging metaphors, they may define an agenda, a plan, or projects for you to develop over many journals to come.

Try a visual representation of the feeling of a journal entry. Start with a small, rich idea plopped in the middle of a page, and spiral it out to the margins in a gyre of color and text. The lists you create may suggest linear patterns of design or ornamentation. If it suits your style, record moments in the color that you associate with an experience or narrative. You can even express an experience with one large, dark word or image on each page.

Applications

In this section, we'll look step by step at 10 sample pages, each featuring a different approach to content. These approaches range from the most familiar and commonly used—information gathering and storytelling—to increasingly reflective and analytic processes, including mining your journal for materials that can be developed into other creative projects.

The choices you make about the content grow directly out of your reasons for keeping a journal or making a scrapbook. You may have chosen to record everything of interest that happens to you each day. Or you might want to focus more narrowly and create an ongoing collection of ideas and images about a particular subject that interests you: ancient music, ferns and mosses, your new baby. By keeping in mind the purpose of the book, you can create beautiful pages that express your intentions both visually and verbally.

Wendy Hale Davis, *Transformer*, 1993. Pen, ink, collage. PHOTO BY BOB DAEMMRICH

 # Information Gathering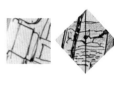

Traditional diarists, logbook keepers, and sketch artists have always used observation and information gathering as a primary approach. Observation is also a favorite tool of researchers in fields such as anthropology and education. When you observe, you simply focus and record whatever you perceive as closely as possible, either in writing or by sketching.

For example, you might have a particular goal or question in mind: What kinds of birds are visiting the bird feeder this week? Or you might set out to record whatever happens around you as you walk through a foreign marketplace or ride a train from one city to another. Observations simply present information. They don't interpret, judge, or ask questions, or reflect. Observation is a process for gathering raw material. After you've made your initial observations, you might choose to go back and reflect on them, but while you're writing or drawing, your only interest, your focus, is on being an instrument that witnesses and records. You can do some recording and observation after an experience, but don't wait too long or you'll forget details. It's best to observe and record on the spot. Next best is to rush home to your journal and catch up before you've forgotten too much. A good compromise is to take very quick, sketchy notes, both visually and verbally, on the spot and then go over your notes, filling in the gaps, as soon as you get home.

Ann Turkle used black pen for her information-gathering entries.

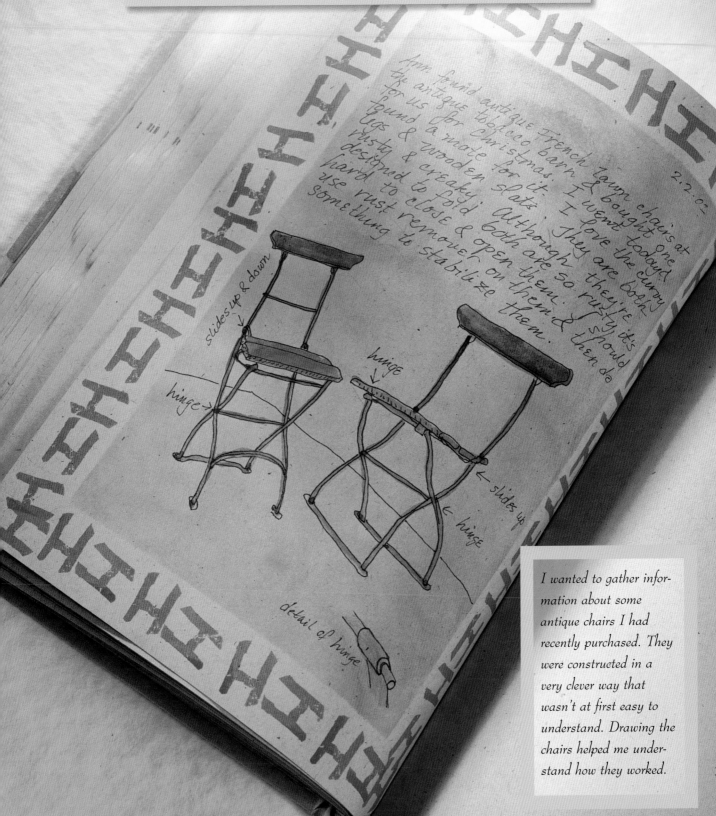

2.2.02

Ann found antique French lawn chairs at the antique tool co barn & bought one for us for Christmas. I went today & found a mate for it. I love the curvy legs & wooden slats. They are both rusty & creaky. Although they're designed to fold, both are so rusty it's hard to close & open them. I should use rust remover on them & then do something to stabilize them.

slides up & down

hinge →

hinge

← slides up

← hinge

detail of hinge

I wanted to gather information about some antique chairs I had recently purchased. They were constructed in a very clever way that wasn't at first easy to understand. Drawing the chairs helped me understand how they worked.

◀ STEP 1

I had prepared a page by sponging on stamp pad ink (see pages 63 to 64). The sunny color of this page suited this journal entry. If the next available page in my journal had been prepared in a way that didn't seem to go with this idea, I would have skipped that page and used the next page that did. Skipped pages are useful for going back and reflecting on entries or further developing them in various ways.

STEP 2 ▶

I chose black waterproof pen to work in because I wanted the crisp, clear detail this kind of pen can give. I decided to use a full-page layout with a border because the written entry was rather short and could fit nicely on the same page as the drawings, making a pleasing and easy-to-understand composition.

I sketched out the chairs lightly, looking very carefully at details, such as the way the legs fold together and bend when the chair is closed. To get the proportions right, I measured the length of the backs of the chairs against their widths. I was careful to draw only what I saw, not what my brain told me about chairs. For example, from where I was sitting, the seats of the chairs looked thin and flattened, rather than square. Had I drawn them as I knew they really were, that is, square, the chairs would have looked strange because from the point of view from which I

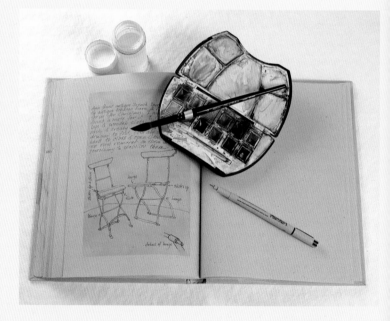

was drawing I could see only the front ends plus a little of the top surfaces of the chairs. It's important in drawing representationally to maintain a uniform point of view. Keep your head still and draw only what you can see from that point of view.

▲ STEP 3

After I had drawn the chairs and the detail of the hinge, I wrote the entry and tried out a watercolor wash on the detail of the hinge.

Since all of the information was gathered in step 2, I could have done step 3 later. I simply added a watercolor wash to the chairs and printed a border using a cork stamp of the letter "H." The shape of the H reminded me of the back of one of the chairs, so I used it as the basis of the pattern that decorates the border.

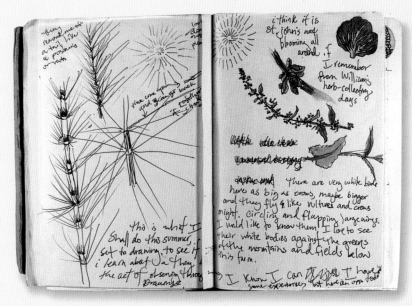

Laura Carter chose black pen highlighted by touches of watercolor to gather detailed information about plants on this page. PHOTO BY ELYSE WEINGARTEN

Storytelling

Storytelling differs from simple information gathering in that when we tell a story, we select details and events that help shape information for a certain purpose. The story can be based on fact or fiction; have a moral or lesson; have a funny or a surprising outcome; or reinforce, present, or question certain cultural ideas or history. Anne Frank's famous diary is essentially a storytelling journal in which each day's entry presents a part of the story of a Jewish family's experience in Germany during World War II.

On these pages, Kelcey Loomer recounts the story of a moonlight swim at the summer solstice through a written entry and painted image. PHOTO BY ELYSE WEINGARTEN

In this page by the author, one side of the entry tells the story verbally, while the other illustrates the event in watercolor and handcarved cork stamp, on a page that was prepared with poured acrylic. PHOTO BY ELYSE WEINGARTEN

Whatever the purpose of a story, it generally has a beginning, a climax, and an ending. The visual counterpart of the story is an illustration. An information-gathering sketch aims at accuracy and clarity. An illustration has a similar relationship to a story. It not only presents information but also evokes certain emotional responses in the viewer. When we draw illustrations, we select details, colors, and a composition that will help tell the story we want to tell. Illustrations and stories can enhance each other or stand on their own.

The field behind & beyond the poggio vecchio has been planted in hay this year. One day we awaken to a distant soft clattering sound. Mowing is going on all over the valley, and today it's happening in the poggio field. Two men are doing the job with a tiny tractor.

By buona sera time the sea of grass has been sheared and lies in sweet smelling waves on the ground. By lunch time the next day the stems have been raked & packed into workmanlike cubic rectangles.

And the next time we trudge past on our way to the alimentari, the hay bricks have been stacked into what looks like a toy barn; & a black plastic tarp has been tied like a handkerchief over the top, morning it to the ground against frequent rain. Fending off the infrequent

In the example shown here, the story was very simple, but it served to tell about a cultural practice in a small village in Italy where I was spending a few weeks. This story doesn't have a great moral point, an exciting development, or a surprise ending, but it does explain the sudden appearance of a curious structure made of hay.

I began on a plain, white, unprepared page. I chose a grid layout because the hay blocks were such a prominent part of the story, and this layout echoed their shape and repetition. Also, writing and drawing in separate blocks echoed the days in the long process I was describing. The first step was to lightly rule off the page with graphite pencil.

◀ STEP 2

Next, I wrote and sketched in the boxes using waterproof black pen because of its clarity and ability to render small details. When I finished, I carefully erased the pencil guidelines I had made in the first step.

STEP 3 ▶

Finally, I used colored pencils to color in the drawings and to make a pattern of wavy, haylike lines over all the spaces that were not written or drawn on. I cut a sunlike shape from a gold foil candy wrapper and glued it to the top of the page to refer to the hot sunny weather necessary for haying.

Lists and Collections

Making a list or recording a collection of items that have something in common are good ways to look at a place or a situation from a slight distance. This process, besides being interesting to do in itself, can lead to longer reflections, or even, if you're so inclined, to stories and poems. The pillow book described on page 100 is an example of a journal that contains many diverse lists and collections.

Pick a category of things that interests you or that you've noticed recurring in your surroundings. Find as many examples as you can in that category. Categories can be attributes, such as "the tastes of different kinds of olives," or objects, such as "doorways," or "plants blooming during May."

Left: Bruce Kremer's lively collection of fish was done using pen and watercolor, with a line of typed text collaged at the bottom.

Right: Kremer incorporated a bird map of New Zealand into his journal to keep track of all the birds he spotted there.

I made a collection of yoga asanas (positions) that are calming. My intention was to use the collection as a reminder. Since I knew how to do the asanas, I didn't need detailed drawings; a simple icon was sufficient. I chose wax resist, using crayons and watercolor because this medium is good for quick gesture drawings that are graceful as well as colorful. Columns were used so the list would be easy to read when I was practicing yoga, but I selected a page that had a graceful poured preparation to lend a dynamic underlayer to the design.

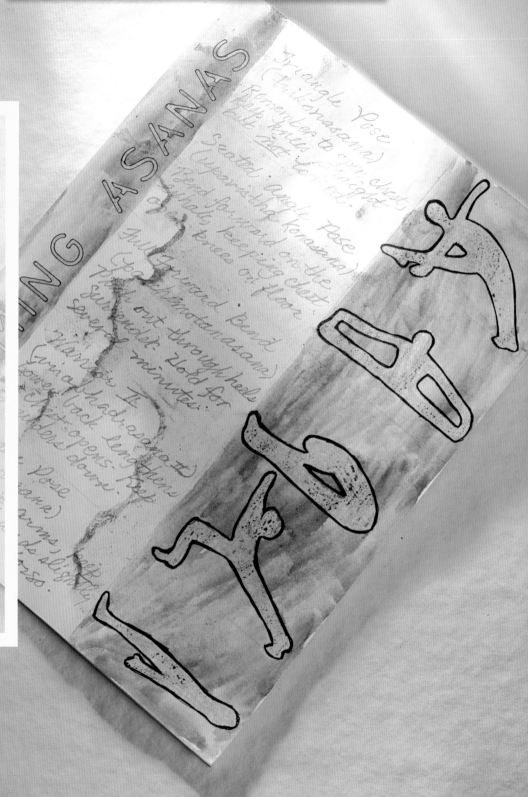

STEP 1

I started with a page that had liquid acrylics poured over it in a flowing design. I used a graphite pencil to lightly rule off columns for each asana and written explanation.

STEP 2 ▶

I then referred to photographs of each asana and drew them with crayons in their boxes. I outlined each figure with waterproof black pen. I wrote explanations and notes on each asana in pencil.

◀ STEP 3

Finally, I brushed a watercolor wash over the drawings to add color and to make the drawings stand out. Then I used a stencil to do the lettering down the left-hand column.

The Pillow Book of Sei Shonagon

Sei Shonagon was a diarist and poet who lived in Japan during the Heian period, a golden age of peace and prosperity in Japanese culture. She was born in 966 and died in 1013. During her lifetime, aristocratic women enjoyed influential roles at court, even though they were excluded from political affairs.

Wit and intelligence and the ability to write letters and poems in fine calligraphy were all desirable attributes among the educated women of the court. Both men and women kept journals which were collections of their thoughts and impressions, character sketches and court gossip, and musings about such topics as the transience of life. It is thought that they kept these journals in their sleeping quarters; hence they came to be known as "pillow books."

Sei Shonagon began writing her journal in an informal notebook style that is known as *makura no soshi*, or pillow book style. Yet even her informal writing was done in such a pure form of prose that it is considered a model of good style. Although she began her journal in private, it was soon circulated at court because of its elegant style and witty, beautifully written contents. Once her book became well known, Shonagon began writing in a more self-conscious manner, with an awareness that her pillow book would be read by the public. She was an excellent and detached observer of her own culture. She

Kano Chikayasu, *Scenes from the Tale of Genji*.

The panels in this screen depict courtly life during Japan's Heian period, the era represented in Shonagon's *Pillow Book*.

used her sharp wit to criticize those she considered beneath her, while at the same time praising the Imperial family.

Shonagon's book is a collection of anecdotes and impressions, but its most striking feature is its 164 lists. These lists, more than any other part of the pillow book, give us a detailed picture of Heian upper-class life, preoccupations, and values. The titles of the lists themselves tell us what was important and worth noticing in this ancient culture. Some of the titles are "Things That Give an Unclean Feeling," "Annoying Things," "Things Which Distract in Moments of Boredom," "Hateful Things," "Rare Things," and "Things Which Make One's Heart Beat Faster."

Shonagon's pillow book was translated into English by Arthur Waley in 1929 and by Ivan Morris in 1967. Amazingly, this very old journal has maintained its appeal, and Morris's translation is still a popular book today. Morris's original translation is in two volumes and is considered the standard complete translation. In 1991 he published an abridged translation in which some of the lists were cut. Following are lists from Morris's 1967 translation:

Elegant Things
– A white coat worn over a violet waistcoat
– Duck eggs
– Shaved ice mixed with liana syrup and put in a new silver bowl
– A rosary of rock crystal
– Wisteria blossoms
– Plum blossoms covered with snow
– A pretty child eating strawberries

Things That Have Lost Their Power
– A large boat which is high and dry in a creek at ebbtide
– A woman who has taken off her false locks to comb the short hair that remains
– A large tree that has been blown down in a gale and lies on its side with its roots in the air
– A man of no importance reprimanding an attendant

Things That Cannot Be Compared
– Summer and winter
– Night and day
– Rain and sunshine
– Youth and age
– A person's laughter and his anger
– Black and white
– Love and hatred

(from *The Pillow Book of Sei Shonagon*, translated and edited by Ivan Morris. New York: Columbia University Press, 1967)

Patterns and Motifs

Patterns and motifs refer to recurring thematic elements. A pattern usually refers to a fixed and regular repetition of shapes or of a single shape, whereas a motif refers to an element that pops up frequently in an environment. Patterns and motifs can be on a micro level, such as shapes that repeat at regular intervals on the surface of a leaf. They can also be on a macro level, such as the pattern of the seasons every year or the pattern of changes that the moon repetitively goes through every 28 days. Naturalists' journals, such as the ones described on page 67, often contain patterns and motifs.

Looking for patterns and motifs in a particular environment or in daily life can give you interesting insights. When you focus on finding them, you begin to find them everywhere. Patterns and motifs tell you something about the structures and order of places, objects, people, and events. You can become aware of visual patterns as well as patterns of speech, cultural patterns, the patterns and motifs that are found in nature, and the patterns that govern so much of your own life.

Andrea A. Peterson, *NY Sketchbook*, 1993. Hemp, pastels, and marker. PHOTO BY ARTIST

The motifs on this page are simplified forms of things found in nature, designs I copied from ceramic artwork in a museum in Italy. Like the artist who rendered these abstracted leaves, pods, and stems, you can simplify patterns and designs from your environment.

In designing the page in this example, I began search-
ing for patterns and motifs in a museum that had a
collection of very old ceramics and other artifacts. I
used a page that had been prepared with a stamped pattern that reminded me of the old brickwork on the
walls of the museum.

◀ STEP 2

While in the museum, I used a black waterproof pen to
sketch motifs and patterns that I found on some of the
ceramics and other objects on display. I also wrote
some observations about the patterns and motifs and
about the pieces themselves. The pen was dark enough
to show up against the pattern of the paper. I used a
small grid to lay out the page because the regularity of
the grid emphasized the regularity of patterns. Because
I was working on site, I wasn't able to rule off the grid
first, but simply scattered the drawings in a more or
less gridlike arrangement.

STEP 3 ▶

When I got home, I added watercolor in a cool,
greenish gray color, something like the color of the
ceramics and a nice contrast with the warm tones
of the brick pattern.

Bird's Eye View

Years ago, people used to draw a kind of map by going up to the tallest hilltop around and drawing the town in the valley as if seen by a bird flying over. These maps were called *bird's-eye* maps. During the 19th century, bird's-eye maps were made for a number of towns in the United States. You can still find examples, such as the one below, in the local history collections of some public libraries or in the Library of Congress. One interesting thing about a bird's-eye map is that it shows more than the unassisted human eye can see, both in terms of breadth of vision and also detail.

For our next approach to content, we'll view a subject as if seeing it from a great distance, but with good detail, like a bird's-eye map. There are several ways of pulling back and getting a broader perspective on your subject. One way to do this is by making a floor plan; another is by mapping. Making diagrams of systems can also accomplish this. Any of these processes can help you get a "big picture" view of a place or a whole system. When you put things together in a system, you begin to understand how the parts function together, as well as what proportion of the system or place is given over to a particular kind of object or activity. Maps and diagrams are also useful planning devices, helping you see your ideas before committing money and time to them.

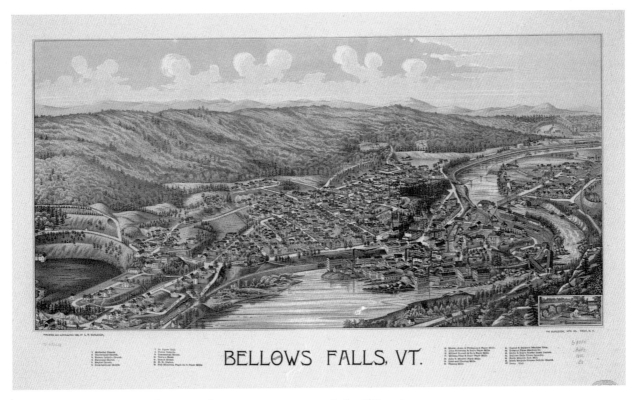

BELLOWS FALLS, VT.

Bird's eye maps, like this one of Bellows Falls, Vermont, were common in the 19th century.

In the example page shown here, I was interested in mapping an ideal garden. I modeled it loosely on a medieval garden plan that I found in a book and modified it to suit the space I had available. Even though I knew I couldn't build such an elaborate garden all at once, having the map was a useful guide as I went about adding elements of the plan to the space.

I began with a page of grid paper that I laminated into a journal. Because the grid paper was rather thin, I knew the stamps I planned to use would bleed through the paper. It made sense to laminate the grid paper to a journal page rather than tip it in because I wanted the protection of a backing page. First, I sketched the location of the different parts of the garden in pencil, including the house, ponds, walls, and all of the plantings.

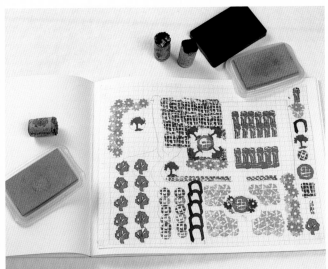

◀ STEP 2

Next, I used stamps that I had carved out of corks and erasers (see page 25) to record the garden areas on the map. The individual stamp designs became interesting patterns when I repeated them.

STEP 3 ▶

I colored the areas between elements with water-soluble colored pencils and brushed over the strokes with water to make washes that retained some stroke marks. Then, I used commercial rubber stamp letters to stamp on the names of the different garden elements and homemade cork alphabet stamps to add the title.

Decision Making

A journal can be a great tool in decision making. Usually when a journaler uses a journal to help decide things, she will simply write. She might make two lists, with the pros and cons of each decision written out in logical fashion. She might write an analysis of each possibility and the ramifications of each choice. These are good processes, but they have one shortcoming; they are mental or logical processes. It's important to go beyond rational and logical thoughts when making decisions. When we omit our emotions or our intuition from the decision-making process, we lose important information. We're so used to valuing the logical in our culture that we often overlook our feelings or consider them to be frivolous or indulgent. But the truth is that if we make a decision that is logical but doesn't satisfy our feelings, we will often regret that decision.

The process of using visual as well as verbal means to compare things helps us discover emotional and intuitive information. The difficult part is finding out what we really feel or sense about something. A useful way to begin is by closing your eyes and visualizing one of the possibilities. Ask yourself what colors and shapes you see. Avoid literally imagining an object, person, or a place. Stick with colors, shapes, sounds, or smells. Then open your eyes and begin to paint or draw, just putting down colors and shapes that reflect what you felt and sensed. When you're satisfied that you've represented your image for the first possibility, repeat the process for the next one.

Amy Cook, from *Relocation Journal*, 2000. Pen and ink, collage. Journal by Dan Essig.

In the example shown here, I was trying to decide which house to buy. I started with unprepared paper because I didn't want to be influenced by any colors or shapes that were already on the page. I used two facing pages, one for each possibility. Watercolors were a good medium because I could work quickly and without thought.

I closed my eyes and visualized the first house. Immediately, I saw morning sunlight playing on a warm wooden floor. I opened my eyes and quickly painted golden yellow shapes against a warm brown background.

◀ STEP 2

I then closed my eyes and imagined the second house. The colors and shapes that came to me were cool, light, and bulky shapes, a feeling of being closed in with a little cool light filtering through. I opened my eyes and painted colors and shapes to describe that image.

When both pages were dry, I made a list on each page of attributes of the paintings, such as "warm, moving, open, light, morning, flow, moving outward, shadows" and "cool, blue, crowded, looming shapes, dark, narrow, soft." I resisted making a decision or even any judgments at this point.

▲ STEP 3

When I had finished the two lists, I began to write sentences about each painting, free-associating things about the paintings, NOT about the houses. For example, I wrote about the first painting, "Dark shapes hold light out, but the light is so penetrating that it leaks into the dark spaces. Upside down, the painting seems to be more about light flowing into a warm, dark space, a comfortable container. The edges where light and dark meet are irregular and uncertain." About the second painting I wrote, "Clunky pillows of color are piled up against a cool, blue opening. The shapes look layered and soft, like pillows, like blankets. Upside down, the shapes seem to hold up the red top part. The blue is an opening directly out into space. There is a clear openness, no barriers, but the pillow shapes look like they could fall down and smother the opening at any time."

In the border around the paintings, I wrote my logical thoughts about each house. It became clear as I wrote that the houses were equal in terms of cost, location, space, and condition. So I left the journal opened to this page on my desk for several days.

Over time I found myself gravitating to the yellow and brown image more and more. In the end, I bought the house that image represented, and lived happily there for many years. Although the other house was a good house, it didn't feel as right to me emotionally as the house I bought. Painting the image helped clarify the hard-to-describe characteristics that I recognized emotionally and intuitively but that hadn't fit into my logical thinking.

MEMORY BOOKS AND MORE

A memory book is a journal-like book that contains carefully selected images that celebrate a specific part of one's life. One forerunner of the memory book is the family Bible, where births, baptisms, marriages, and deaths were entered in the margins and on the flyleaves. Such Bibles became a kind of family memory book. Sometimes, photographs as well as birth, marriage, baptismal, and death certificates were pasted in, resulting in true altered books that contain a history of a family. In some cases these are the only records left of a family, and altered Bibles have become legal documents.

Many early memory books centered around children and family. By the early 20th century, these had been commercialized, and people could buy already-formatted books that had drawings of idealized babies and nursery items, along with blank spaces in which the record-keeper could write the baby's weight, height, first words, first toys, and other firsts. There were pages for reflection and description, and pages devoted to photographs and other memorabilia—cards, school papers, old report cards, the little envelope of hair from the first haircut.

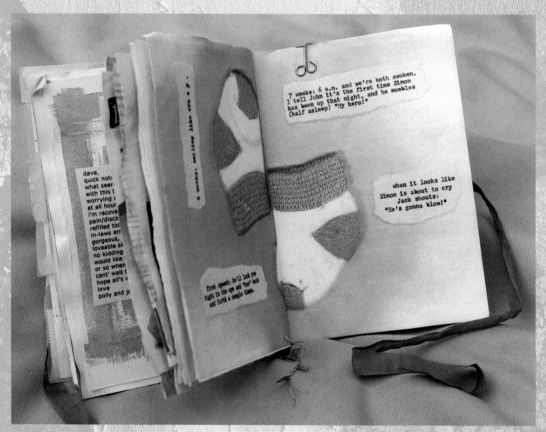

Polly Smith, *Simon*, 2000-2001. Color photocopies, mementos, photographs, watercolor, and collage.
PHOTO BY ARTIST

Beata Wehr, *My Home=My Homes*,
1997. Collage, painting, pen, and ink.
PHOTO BY ARTIST

High school memory books were soon commercialized also, and these followed the format of baby books—sentimental illustrations decorating pages with blanks left for specific information. Many of us still have these albums, bulging with dried corsages and party napkins, filled with exhortations from our friends to "Have a great life and remember ME!"

The main difference between a memory book and a journal is that a journal, whatever its focus, is inclusive of the good and the bad, the momentous and the trivial, the beautiful and the not so beautiful. Memory books, on the other hand, are focused on a particular person, event, or brief time period, and their makers tend to select certain positive aspects of the event or person to remember. In addition, memory books, because of their element of selectivity, are usually made after the fact and are designed and structured to fit their particular purposes, whereas journals are works in progress, with each day's entry simply being made on the next available page.

Journals can and often do furnish raw material for memory books. Going back into a journal to look for patterns and trends, themes and repetitions can be one of the great pleasures of journal-keeping. A memory book made to celebrate a particular event might recast images and written passages from a journal, as well as include materials that weren't included in the original journal, such as photographs.

If the makers of memory books tend to select and shape the raw material from journals and other sources, artists who make what are called *bookworks* or *artists' books* go a step further. Artists' books, or bookworks, are difficult to define, but artist Ulises Carrion gave a good definition when he said, "Bookworks are books that are conceived as an expressive unity, that is to say, where the message is the sum of all materials and formal elements." (Ulises Carrion. *Second Thoughts*. Amsterdam: Void Distributors, 1980: 25.) Journals can be made to fit virtually any container,

from a dime-store notebook to a handmade, leather-bound book. Yet the form and materials of an artists' book are integral to its expression, and the forms of artists' books are as varied, yet specific to the concept, as those of any other sculptural form. One distinguishing characteristic of an artists' book is that its folds and cuts, the way it is opened and manipulated, and the materials used in its construction all carry meaning.

Book artists use the material from journals to make books, but these books go beyond the scope of memory books in that they raise questions as well as give information about people and events. Many artists' books involve memory, but the interest of the artists is more in the subject of memory and its place in our lives than in celebrating a particular memory. Even those books devoted to a particular memory often tease apart the layers of memories and contrast different people's memories of the same person or event. Like all postmodern artwork, bookworks question assumptions and open our eyes to new possibilities.

Journals, memory books, and artists' books are distinct genres; but they all grow out of the common practices of paying close attention, of selecting parts of an experience to remember, and of transforming experiences into visual and verbal expression.

Spilling

Journals are often used for the expression of emotions, both in writing and visually. "Spilling" is a term coined by writing teachers for the process of free writing at the beginning of a class session. When students spill, they pour their emotions out onto the paper with no attention to grammar, spelling, or the niceties of composition. The purpose is to empty the emotions, to clear the mind. Spilling can also be done visually, by painting, collaging, or drawing colors and shapes that express emotions. The person constructing this kind of visual is not concerned with appearance or with perfect composition and technique. Colors and shapes are chosen for their emotionally evocative qualities. They are laid down quickly, without giving the ever-judging mind a chance to intervene.

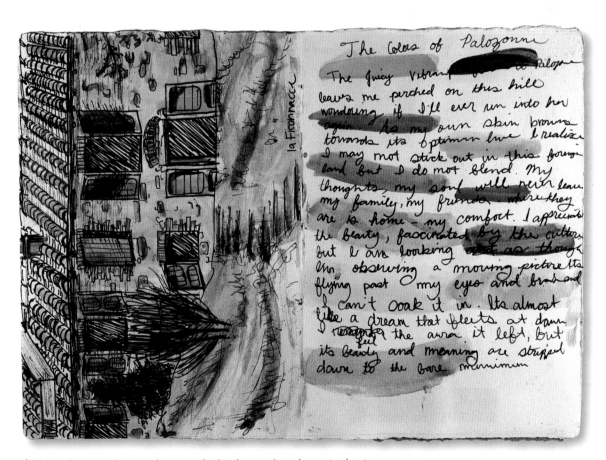

Blair Gulledge used watercolor to emphasize the emotions she wrote about. PHOTO BY ELYSE WEINGARTEN

In this example, I was concerned with expressing the sense of bewilderment and helplessness that I felt when I was immersed in a foreign language at an intensive language learning program.

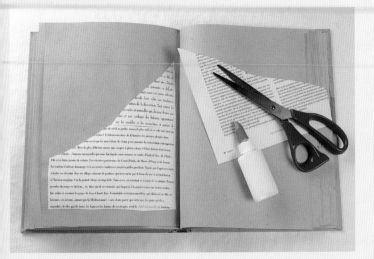

◀ STEP 1

I began with an unprepared page to which I glued a cutout of foreign language text. I shaped the cutout and glued it in such a way as to divide the page along a diagonal, because I wanted the feeling of instability that this layout can give.

STEP 2 ▶

I wrote my feelings about the situation in wax crayon across the whole page, covering the collaged part as well as the top of the page. Then I quickly painted over the page with watercolor. Because the collage paper was glossy, I added a small amount of dishwashing detergent to the watercolor. The detergent breaks the surface tension of the water and allows it to attach itself to the glossy paper, on which it would otherwise bead. Besides helping the paint stick to the page, the detergent gave an interesting foamy texture to the paint.

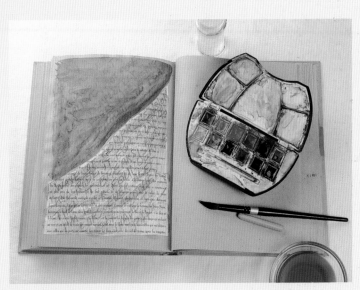

◀ STEP 3

Finally, I cut out a small paper boat from glossy magazine paper and glued it in position. I drew over a few of the words with a dark colored pencil in order to emphasize them.

Changing Forms

Changing a form in the context of a journal means simply to record visually and in writing what you can hear, smell, taste, or touch. Changing the form of a sensation or perception deepens your experience of the original, making it fuller and richer. This visual record of a fleeting sensation or perception makes it possible to remember an experience that might otherwise be lost.

To change the form of a sensation, you need to focus intently, so you not only hear a particular distant soft clattering sound, but you associate a color and shape with it, thereby fleshing out the sound and implanting it more fully in your memory. The nostalgic odor of a lilac bush takes on a shape as well as color. The myriad tastes of young vegetables fresh from a garden become a pattern of colors moving in a shape that awakens your senses to the original every time you look at it.

This collection of sounds by the author was rendered visually using crayon resist. PHOTO BY ELYSE WEINGARTEN

For this page, I took my naturalist's journal for a walk at a bird sanctuary on a warm day in July. I represented the sounds I heard with colors, shapes, and patterns.

STEP 1 ▶

I began with a page that had been prepared by sponging on stamp pad ink in a shape that reminded me of the organic form of a pond.

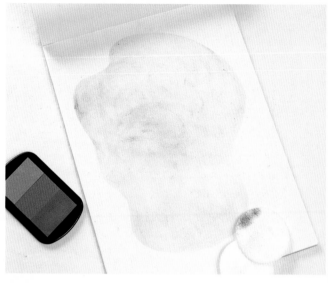

◀ STEP 2

I stood in one place and closed my eyes and let the sounds arrive on the soft breeze. The longer I listened, the easier it became to isolate different sounds. I began to focus on one in particular, and soon I saw a particular shade of yellow every time I heard the sound. The sound was liquid and trilling, seeming to form an elongated puddle that trailed off as it faded. I recorded the sound by sketching in a puddle shape in pencil and by making written notes about the color. It would have been convenient to have a small set of colored pencils, but written color notes work well, too. I then focused on another sound and repeated the recording process. I continued focusing and recording until I was satisfied that I had gathered a good collection of the sounds of the bird sanctuary on that day.

◀ STEP 3

When I got home, I painted in each shape using white gouache in order to overcome the background color. When the gouache dried, I colored over the shapes with colored pencils. I let the field notes that I had made stand, as they added interesting written as well as visual information.

"Songcatcher" Journal

Elizabeth Ellison is an artist who lives in the mountains of western North Carolina. When the movie "Songcatcher" (Trimark Pictures, 2000) was being shot in her hometown, Elizabeth was commissioned to do some watercolor paintings for use in the film. In order to get the right feeling and look to her paintings, she needed to understand and empathize with the character, a woman named Alice, who was supposed to have painted the watercolors. Elizabeth had several conversations with the director of the movie, with the actor who played Alice, and with several other actors. She spent several days visiting the set, making some paintings, and taking some photographs of the location.

Throughout the project, Elizabeth kept a journal filled with notes and paintings as an aid to focusing and deepening her experience. She wrote her speculations about what the character's life would be like, what kinds of things she would want to paint, and what kinds of materials and techniques her life situation would make possible. She made small watercolor sketches of scenes and objects that would be in Alice's immediate environment. She also wrote about the movie-making process and her impressions of the people she worked with. Elizabeth used a journal that she made herself out of sheets of paper made partly from plants that Alice would have known.

Each page of the journal is an elegant balance of visual and verbal material. On one page, the watercolor that has been attached to the page has a small hole in the top. Elizabeth noted in her text entry that the hole was from the nail that was used to hang the painting to the wall of the cabin during the filming of scenes in Alice's home.

This journal is very good demonstration of the power of a visual-verbal journal not only to document a project but to deepen the journaler's focus and learning during the experience. It is also a perfect example of a journal that serves as a springboard for a later creative project (see page 122).

Elizabeth Ellison, *Songcatcher Journal*, 1999. Watercolor, pen and ink.

The material in a journal, album, or scrapbook is an invaluable stockpile of ideas and images that you can mine for future creative projects. An interesting alchemy seems to take place inside a journal over time, so that when you dip back into the book, you often see the exact image you need or the perfect phrase to jump-start a piece of writing. In this way, today's unpromising journal entry might show up transformed as tomorrow's poem, essay, painting, or artist's book. Artist Elizabeth Ellison's journal, featured in the essay on page 121, was her springboard to making paintings for the movie "Songcatcher."

Some people date the spines or covers of their journals and write titles reflecting the contents with the idea of using their journals in the future. Others go back through completed journals and number the pages, then use sticky notes to write the topics that are included on certain pages. The topic labels sticking out of the journal fore edge make it easy to index the journal. The journaler need only write the number of the page on which the topic appears on the sticky note. Then she or he can gather all the sticky notes, alphabetize them, and write the topics and page numbers in the back of the journal, perhaps on the inside back cover.

Robert Johnson, *Notebook Page*, 1998. Manuel Antonio, Costa Rica, Agouti capuchin monkeys; watercolor and graphite on paper. Collection of Gwen Diehn

Robert Johnson uses his sketchbook journals to collect images for his full-scale paintings.

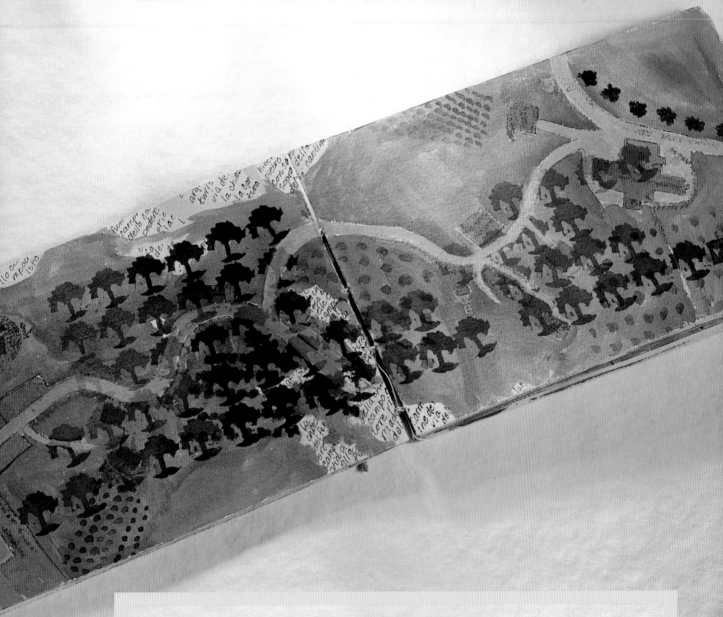

In the journal page seen here, I wanted to make an artists' book about the experience of being in a place where I couldn't speak the language or understand much about the culture. I wanted to convey my sense of confusion (not being able to understand or be understood, my disorientation) but also my great appreciation for the beauty of the place.

In going back through my travel journal from the place, I found some pages of maps that I had drawn, as well as some cork stamp prints of patterns and motifs. I also found pages where I had written and drawn about the language situation.

◀ STEP 1

First, I bound the book and prepared pages with poured acrylic. I made photocopies of the map pages, then transferred them to heavy drawing paper with citrus-based paint stripper (see pages 66 to 68).

STEP 2 ▶

Next, I used watercolors to paint areas around and on the map in greens, reds, and tan. I didn't strictly follow the lines of the map but painted in a more interpretive way, using the map as more of a shape than a literal map. I added some patterns that reminded me of the agricultural patterns in the landscape.

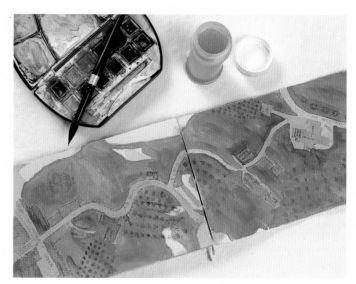

◀ STEP 3

One of the last steps was to use a cork stamp of a tree to print tree patterns over the map and the "countryside." Finally, I copied some Italian text, using pen. I wrote the text as though it were an underlayer, allowing it to disappear in mid-word as it slid under painted edges. I followed a similar process for the other pages in the book.

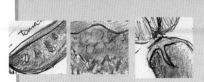

Reflections

Another popular use for journals is to reflect on experiences, helping a journaler to make inferences and judgments about places, events, and people. Of course, reflections are often a part of other kinds of journal entries too. But sometimes reflection is the primary purpose of an entry.

My friends Susan and Jeff have kept a journal of reflections and memories of all the dinners they have given for friends during the long years of their marriage. At the end of a fine evening, they will pull out the journal and its accompanying box of colored pencils, paints, and pens. They then invite their guests to document the event by writing and drawing in the journal. Many of the pages are collaborations, as each guest draws items from the menu and writes comments about the evening. Sometimes people glue in wine labels. Some people retell jokes or write comments on the food. Susan and Jeff often write the menu and some of the recipes, and then they write ideas to make particular foods better, or to improve future picnics or holidays.

Susan and Jeff Griesmaier, page from *Dinner Party Book, 1998.*

125

I wanted to create a visual record of a memorable picnic. I chose crayons and watercolor to convey the informal feel of the day, and used a mandala layout so I could include many different aspects of the event centered around the main reflection: the meal.

In this journal page, I began with a two-page spread that had been prepared by pouring liquid acrylics into the fold of the page, giving a more or less symmetrical underlayer—a good beginning for a mandala layout.

◀ STEP 2

The next step was to draw the food that was served at the picnic, arranging the items in a mandala centered around the bowl of soup. I used watercolor crayons.

STEP 3 ▶

To finish the reflection, I brushed water over the crayons to turn the strokes into washes. Then I used graphite pencil to sketch the tablecloth pattern and painted it in with watercolors. I also used watercolor to darken the color of the bowl of soup since its original color looked too similar to the blue of the tablecloth. The final step was to write reflections on the picnic in pen. I slanted the writing and made it seem to go under the tablecloth in places to add to the impression of a layer.

ACKNOWLEDGMENTS

Boundless thanks to Dusty Benedict for conversations over many years during which the idea for this book was first hatched; and to Ann Turkle for preparing the section on writing, and for collaborating with me to develop the processes as well as the concepts set forth in the book. Thanks as always to my journal-keeping students at Warren Wilson College, who never fail to astound me with their ability and imagination.

I especially thank all those who allowed me to use pages from their journals as examples (see Contributing Artists below for a full list).

Thanks also to those who waded through early drafts as well as later ones and managed to give me constructive criticism while still being encouraging: Dusty Benedict, Rebecca Casey, Kristie Diehn, Susan Griesmaier, and Ann Turkle. And thanks to Elyse Weingarten for her excellent supplementary photography.

There cannot be a better group of people to work with than the editorial team at Lark who put this book together. Thanks to Joanne O'Sullivan for being a peerless editor, sensitive and smart as well as unfailingly optimistic and superb at keeping things organized; to Rain Newcomb for tracking down difficult-to-find images and information; to Deborah Morgenthal for astute observations and great good humor; to Evan Bracken for being able to work small miracles with photography; to Celia Naranjo for pulling so many disparate pieces together into a cohesive and beautiful book design; and to Carol Taylor for being the book's champion from the beginning.

CONTRIBUTING ARTISTS

Laurie Adams

Nina Bagley

Coranna Beene

Dusty Benedict

Laura Carter

Amy Cook

Sheila Cunningham

Wendy Hale Davis

David Diehn

Elizabeth Ellison

Dan Essig

Susan Kaupsinski Gaylord

Susan and Jeff Griesmaier

Blair Gulledge

Charlotte Hayes

Dorothy Herbert

Hannah Hinchman

Coral Jensen

Robert Johnson

Bruce Kremer

Mary Ellen Long

Kelcey Loomer

Karen Michel

Bobbe Needham

Joseph Osina

Andrea A. Peterson

Susan Saling

Polly Smith

Colleen Stanton

Jenny Taliadoros

Christine Toriello

Ann Turkle

Kerstin Vogdes

Beata Wehr

Pamela Lyle Westhaver

Jennifer Wing

INDEX